Animals Alive

DK

LONDON, NEW YORK, MUNICH,
MELBOURNE, and DELHI

Project editor Wendy Horobin
Project designer Clare Marshall
Editors Lee Wilson, Holly Beaumont, Lorrie Mack
Designers Claire Patané, Hedi Hunter, Karen Hood
US editor Margaret Parrish
Picture researcher Myriam Mégharbi
Production editor Clare McLean
Production controller Claire Pearson
Jacket designers Natalie Godwin, Rachael Grady
Publishing manager Bridget Giles
Art director Martin Wilson
Creative director Jane Bull
Publisher Mary Ling

Consultant Professor Brian Groombridge

First published in the United States in 2011 by
DK Publishing
375 Hudson Street, New York, New York 10014

Copyright © 2011 Dorling Kindersley Limited

11 12 13 14 15 10 9 8 7 6 5 4 3 2 1
178364–01/11

A catalog record for this book
is available from the Library of Congress.

ISBN: 978-0-7566-7213-3

Color reproduction by MDP, UK
Printed and bound in China by Toppan

Discover more at
www.dk.com

Contents

4...........Animals alive!

6...........How animals evolved

8...........The variety of life

10.........Unexpected consequences

12.........Going, going, gone!

14.........What are the threats?

16.........How threatened is it?

18 ....**MAMMALS**

20.........Jaguar

24.........Sumatran orangutan

26.........Sea otter

28.........Ethiopian wolf

30.........Manatee

32.........Tasmanian devil

34.........Polar bear

36.........Black rhinoceros

38 ....**BIRDS**

40.........Southern rockhopper

42.........Whooping crane

46 ....**REPTILES**

48.........Leatherback turtle

50.........Komodo dragon

52 ....**AMPHIBIANS**

54.........Golden toad

56 ....**FISH**

58.........Southern bluefin tuna

60 ....**INVERTEBRATES**

62.........Coral reef

64.........Monarch butterfly

66.........Saving species

68.........Tracking tigers

70.........Keeping animals alive

72.........Backyard naturalist

74.........Setting up a reserve

76.........New species

78.........Glossary

79.........Index

80.........Acknowledgments

Animals alive!

Animals come in **every shape, size, and color.**
They **roam the land**, SWIM IN WATER, and **fly in the air.**
There are **millions** of **different** ANIMALS and every one
has its **own role** to play in the natural world.

To survive, every animal needs **food**, SHELTER, **water**,
and **living space**. The place where it finds these is known
as its habitat. **Habitats** can be as **small as a muddy puddle**
OR as **vast as an ocean**. Some animals can only live in very
specific habitats, while others can live almost anywhere.

What do animals need to **survive?**

Food
Animals need food to provide them with both nutrients and energy. If there is plenty of food available in a habitat it can support a large and healthy population of animals. If the food supply is seasonal or affected by the lifestyle of another species, an animal may have to follow the food and move to a new location.

Shelter
Every animal needs somewhere safe to hide away. This may be to escape from bad weather or predators, to sleep, or to give birth to their young in safety. Without some kind of shelter, animals are vulnerable to death from exposure or they may become dinner for another animal.

Water
Most animals need water to drink, but some get all they need from their food. Amphibians and a number of reptiles also spend part of their lives in water. In desert areas, the ability to make do with only a small amount of water plays a vital role in the animal's lifestyle.

FACT: Animals divide into two groups—those with a backbone

> IT IS NOT THE STRONGEST OF THE SPECIES THAT SURVIVES, NOR THE MOST INTELLIGENT THAT SURVIVES. IT IS THE ONE THAT IS THE MOST ADAPTABLE TO CHANGE.
> **Charles Darwin**

There are thought to be more than **1.3 million** different species of insect on Earth.

On the move

What makes animals different from plants and fungi is the ability to move from one place to another. Even underwater species that attach themselves to rocks spend part of their lives floating freely.

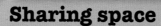

Living space

All animals need space in which to live, but the amount of space needed varies. Some invertebrate animals can live in tiny spaces, while a Siberian tiger needs around 120 square miles (300 square kilometers) in which to roam. Lack of space can lead to overcrowding, competition for food, and the easy spread of diseases.

Sharing space

Each habitat can support only a limited number of species and every species adapts itself to suit a particular role in that habitat. By eating different foods or making its home in a different place, a species can reduce the competition it faces from other animals, yet live side by side with them.

Moving on

If a habitat changes, the animals that live there will have to adapt to the changes or move elsewhere to keep from dying out. They may face competition in their new home from the animals that already live there, and if the habitat can't support any more animals then numbers will go down until they reach a balance.

(vertebrates) and those without a backbone (invertebrates).

How animals **evolved**

If scientists' best estimates that there are up to 10 million animal species LIVING on this planet are correct, where have they all come from and why are there so many? **And why do some species survive while others perish?**

The answers lie in a process of change **called evolution.**

This was the idea of a naturalist named Charles Darwin. He made a five-year trip around the world, collecting and listing the animals and plants he found in each country. He noticed that there were slight differences in the way some of the animals in each species looked or behaved. He wondered whether these differences would give them an advantage over other members of the species if the environment changed, or if they had to move to a new habitat? In time, these differences might even become permanent and result in a completely new species.

How did it all **begin?**

When Earth first formed it was a hostile place. The atmosphere was poisonous and the land was incredibly hot. Life began 3.5 billion years ago as tiny cells that lived in the ocean. Gradually, some of these evolved into soft-bodied worm and jellylike animals. Then, around 540 million years ago, an explosion of new life-forms suddenly began to appear.

630 million years

The first animals lived in the sea. These early soft-bodied invertebrates included sponges, worms, and mollusks. Many had strange shapes and features that are no longer seen.

The first cells lived in hot seawater.

540 million years

As time went on, corals, jawless fish, and arthropods (animals with a segmented, external skeleton) appeared, followed by the first bony fish and sharks.

400 million years

Some fish began to walk on their fins and ventured onto the land. These were the first tetrapods, the ancestors of all four-limbed animals. Tetrapods became amphibians and then reptiles.

These Galápagos finches have all developed different beaks so they can feed on different foods. This enables them to live together without competing for the same food supply.

Ancient ancestors

Darwin loved fossils. He knew that new layers of rock are laid down on top of older layers, and that each layer usually has different fossils. Darwin noted that some animals were found only in old rocks and had no living relatives, while fossils in younger rocks were increasingly similar to living animals. He saw the evolution of life like a tree: some branches (or species) would only grow so far and come to an end in the past, while others would keep dividing and reach up to the present day.

This frog has evolved a long, sticky tongue to catch flying insects.

Adapt and survive

Many animals, such as frogs, produce hundreds of babies every year, but very few of them survive to produce young themselves. Darwin realized that any adaptations that helped an animal survive and reproduce as the environment changed would become common in later generations. He called this idea natural selection.

Insects walked onto the land and then grew wings and began to fly as flowering plants started to take over the land.

10 thousand years

350 million years

200 million years

65 million years

From reptiles came some of the biggest animals ever to have lived—the dinosaurs, and their flying and swimming relatives the pterosaurs and ichthyosaurs.

Birds are thought to have evolved from small, feathery dinosaurs. Tiny nocturnal mammals also began to appear. When dinosaurs and many other species became extinct 65 million years ago, mammals quickly filled the spaces they had left behind.

Without the dinosaurs, mammals grew to be the biggest animals on the planet. Many of the largest ones died out during an ice age 10,000 years ago, leaving one animal to reign supreme—humans.

The variety of life

There are very few places on Earth where you won't find some kind of ANIMAL. No matter how harsh or extreme the **environment**, it is home to a number

How many species?

Estimating how many species there are on Earth is tricky. There are still **large parts** of the world that **haven't been explored** fully and no one knows exactly what lives there. Scientists think there could be anything between 2 million and 100 million species, although most think **10 million** is the best guess. Out of these, only **1.8 million** have been named.

Could there be a new species just **here?**

Ecosystems

We call plants and animals that live **together** in a particular environment an **ecosystem**. Scientists may study the whole of a huge ecosystem, or just part of it. **All** of the plants and animals that live there need or depend on other species to **survive**.

A coral reef is one of the most diverse types of ecosystem. As the reef grows it attracts more species.

Hundreds of different species make their homes among the coral. Each is a food source for another species. If the coral dies, the ecosystem will collapse and the species that live there will change.

FACT: When **scientists** looked closely at **19 trees** in a Panama

of **creatures** that have adapted to live there. We call the variety of plants and animals in an area its **BIODIVERSITY**.

Why is biodiversity important?

Most ecosystems can cope with losing one or two species, but **some species are vital** to the survival of their ecosystem. Over millions of years, animals have **adapted to suit a particular space** in the environment. Like pieces in a jigsaw puzzle, each species interlocks with others. We may not notice any effect if one or two of the pieces are removed, but often we do not know which are the **key pieces**, or what will happen if we lose them. We may be losing species that are vital for our own survival. This may be because they are helping to keep the **planet healthy,** or because they may be of use as a future source of medicine or chemicals.

Hotspots

The number and variety of animals is **not** spread evenly around the world. The **colder regions** around the poles have fewer species than the warm tropical areas around the equator. Some areas, often in forested hills or mountains, are **rich in species** compared with the rest of the region, or have species that are found nowhere else. These are called **hotspots**. Certain areas of the ocean also have a higher number of species than are found elsewhere. Setting up parks and reserves within hotspots can be a good way to help maintain **world biodiversity**.

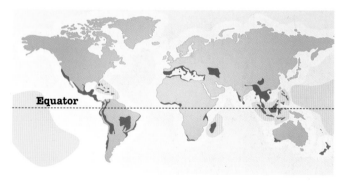

Equator

Land—a large number of plants and animals that live in these regions are not found elsewhere.

Oceans—underwater hotspots are threatened by overfishing and pollution.

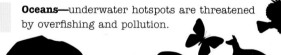

rain forest they found **1,200 different species**... of beetle!

Unexpected consequences

Every animal has a role to play in its ECOSYSTEM. If you remove **one species** the effects might not be **immediately obvious**, but it may eventually have an impact on the **survival** of ANOTHER ANIMAL or **plant**.

The loss of a predator

Yellowstone National Park in the US used to have a large number of gray wolves, but intensive hunting by ranchers meant that by 1925 there were no wolves left.

For 70 years the park was wolf-free. During this time, the ecosystem changed dramatically and many species were affected in unexpected ways. The balance of nature had been upset and the decision was made to bring the wolf back.

Gray wolves were reintroduced to the park in 1995. Since then, the elk and coyote populations have decreased and aspens and willow trees are growing again. Beavers have returned, and grizzly bears and other scavengers have also come back. The wolves are reducing the need for humans to manage the park's elk herds and habitats.

Elk

Gray wolf

Visit the wolves

Wolves

Wolves prey on elk. They mainly take old and sick animals and keep the elk population in check. The carcass remains they leave behind provide food for scavengers, such as eagles, grizzly bears, foxes, and weasels.

Elk

Without the wolves, the number of elk began to rise. Elk browse on aspen and willow trees and with more elk in the park the number of trees began to decrease. Without enough trees to browse, the elk began to starve during the winters.

Gray wolves are predators. They sit at the top of the food chain in many ecosystems because nothing else preys on them. They prefer to eat elk, deer, and wild pigs. Wolves also take farm livestock, which brings them into conflict with humans. As a result, wolves have been killed and driven out of many of their natural ranges.

Beaver

Coyote

Aspen trees
Aspens are a key part of this ecosystem, but if young trees are overbrowsed by elk they may not grow to maturity. Conifers then take over.

Grizzly bear

Mountain bluebird

Beavers

Beavers also depend on aspens and willows, for food and for their dams. By clearing trees, beavers create open habitats for other plants to grow, and their dams improve water quality for fish. As conifers replaced aspens, beavers vanished and the park's ecosystem suffered.

Grizzly bears

Grizzlies prey on elk calves and eat the carrion left by wolves, but they also depend on plants and fish for food. Without the beavers to clear the trees, new shrubs and bushes struggled to grow. The waterways also had fewer fish, and the bears couldn't find enough to eat.

Coyotes

Coyotes took over as the top predator when the wolves disappeared. This caused the number of other scavengers to fall, since coyotes also feed on rodents and smaller game animals. Coyotes prey on deer fawns, and their numbers dropped as the coyotes increased.

Birds

Birds need trees for nesting, shelter, and food. Without the aspens and willows to provide a suitable habitat, many bird species left the park.

Going, going, **gone!**

Extinction is when a species dies out, when the last adults die and leave no young. But it's not all bad—the loss of one species may leave room for another to survive and diversify.

Extinction is natural

Extinction has been a part of life on Earth for as long as life has existed. All life, including plants, animals, and bacteria, has evolved over the last four billion years to give us the world we live in today. For every extinct species, another has adapted and survived.

Unnatural extinction

Most recent extinctions are the result of human activity. Humans hunt animals for food and sport, and dramatically alter the landscape around them. Because we are changing the world so quickly, threatened species don't have a chance to adapt.

The sixth mass extinction

When a single species dies out it often goes unnoticed and has little immediate impact on the rest of the planet. However, scientists know that on five occasions in Earth's history, a huge number of species were wiped out at the same time. These mass extinctions resulted from natural events, such as asteroids hitting Earth, climate change, or volcanic eruptions. Experts now think we are in the middle of a sixth extinction event that is being caused by just one species—humans.

FACT: Experts think that species are becoming extinct up to

Dead and buried

We know that many different creatures inhabited our planet in the past because their remains have been found buried in rocks. These are called fossils. Fossils are important because we can scientifically date the rocks they are found in and this can reveal when different kinds of animal appeared and disappeared—and the pattern of life over millions of years.

> " Scientists estimate that **99 percent** of all the species that have ever lived on Earth have become extinct. That adds up to roughly a billion species that have lived and died since life began. "

As **dead** as a **dodo**

The dodo is the most famous extinction caused by humans. A relative of the pigeon, the dodo lived on the island of Mauritius in the Indian Ocean. When Europeans arrived on the island in 1598, they found the birds to be unafraid of people—and very meaty. This made them sitting targets for the stew pot. Dodos were flightless birds, so even if they learned to avoid their hunters, they could not move out of reach far enough or fast enough. The settlers also brought with them new animals—dogs, cats, and rats—that ate the birds, their eggs, and chicks. Within 80 years, the dodo was extinct.

1,000 times faster than normal because of humans.

What are the threats?

There is ONE **ANIMAL** that is so successful it is putting all other species in DANGER OF EXTINCTION—the human. **There are currently an estimated 6.7 billion people living on the planet**, and **four** new ones are born every second.

Like other animals, **humans need food, shelter, water**, and **room to live**, but we take more of these resources than any other creature. **This is having a huge impact on Earth's other inhabitants**. We are also **damaging the environment** by polluting the AIR, **land**, and **water**, making what little space there is left difficult for animals to live in.

These are some of the main threats that

Habitat loss

This is the biggest problem facing most animals. Clearing land for agriculture, building, or mining often breaks up large stretches of forest or grassland so that only small islands remain. This makes it hard for animals to establish a territory, find enough food, or even find a mate.

Climate change

The effects of climate change are already beginning to be seen. Deserts are spreading, glaciers and ice caps are melting, and sea levels are rising. Unless animals can move to more favorable conditions or adapt quickly, their numbers may decrease or they may even perish.

Hunting

Even protected species are at risk from illegal hunting and poaching. Many animals are taken as bushmeat for food; for their skins, feathers, or horns; for use in traditional medicines; sold as pets; or are destroyed as pests.

No one knows how many species we are losing every year, but some scientists estimate it could be as many as **30,000**.

Natural hazards

Not all threats to animals are man-made, although some may be the result of an accident or an unexpected consequence. Forest and bushfires often break out in hot and dry regions, killing plant life and animals that cannot escape quickly. Other natural events include floods, tsunamis, earthquakes, and volcanoes.

are affecting the lives of **animals:**

Food supply

If a food source shrinks or vanishes, creatures higher up or lower down the food chain will be affected. If a species from the middle of the chain disappears, top predators may not be able to find enough food to survive. Species lower down the food chain may also explode in numbers if there is no predator to keep their numbers in check.

Pollution

Pouring pollutants into the atmosphere, rivers, and oceans, and onto land can disrupt and damage natural environments. Many rivers are polluted with pesticides, industrial waste, and sewage, which deprives fish and animals of oxygen. Waste gases pumped into the air are the main cause of climate change.

Disease

Sudden outbreaks of disease can have a huge impact on species. If an animal is already under stress through habitat loss or climate change, it may not be able to fight off illness. Many amphibians are currently being wiped out by a fungal infection, and honeybees have been suffering from a mysterious illness.

How threatened is it?

How do you tell how endangered an animal is? Very few of Earth's species have been investigated thoroughly. It is only by finding out as much as possible about an animal that scientists can decide how much of a threat it faces.

Biologists study foxes on islands off California.

To work out whether an animal is at risk, experts try to gather data on how its population is changing. For most species this is difficult, so they use information on where the animal lives, the size and quality of its habitat, whether the creature is being exploited for food or body parts, and other threats. Countries often have their own ways of assessing this risk, but at a global level the International Union for the Conservation of Nature (IUCN) has developed a system of nine risk categories.

Near Threatened

NT

These animals are in some danger, but at present **there are enough of them to survive** and they have plenty of good-quality habitat. This doesn't mean they're safe, however—a sudden outbreak of disease might kill many of the adults. This is especially dangerous in species that take a long time to reach breeding age or produce only a few babies.

Vulnerable

VU

This is the first "threatened" category. "Vulnerable" means that animals in the wild are under serious threat because their numbers have dropped dramatically (by as much as half over 10 years), their living space is shrinking into small and separate areas, or their habitat has been badly damaged. There may be fewer than 10,000 adults left.

Endangered

EN

These animals have **a very high risk of extinction in the wild.** Numbers may have fallen by more than half, or the area they live in has been reduced dramatically or split up into areas of less than 200 square miles (500 square kilometers). With some animals in this category there may be fewer than 250 breeding adults left.

Malayan Sun bear

Lesser flamingos

Chimpanzee

Sacred kingfishers are classed as Least Concern.

More than **one-fifth** of vertebrate animals assessed by IUCN are threatened with extinction.

There are three other categories: Least Concern (LC), Data Deficient (DD), and Not Evaluated.

Least Concern—experts have carried out a number of surveys but have decided that the species is not threatened.

Data Deficient—not enough is known about the species to classify it. However, this does not mean it is not at risk.

Not Evaluated—no surveys have been carried out to find out whether the species is threatened.

Spotted seals are described as Data Deficient.

CR

Critically Endangered

This is the **last category before the animal becomes extinct** in its natural habitat. Its numbers may have gone down to 10 percent of what they were, and there may be only one group left in an area of less than 4 square miles (10 square kilometers). There are usually fewer than 50 breeding adults still alive.

EW

Extinct in the Wild

Sometimes no animals of a particular species can be found in their natural habitat—**the only surviving animals are in captivity** in breeding centers or animal sanctuaries elsewhere. Scientists make regular surveys of the original habitat to make sure that no animals have been missed.

EX

Extinct

If an animal has not been seen anywhere in its natural habitat for several generations, and there are none in captivity, the animal is extinct—it's disappeared completely. Scientists still keep looking—the fact that it hasn't been seen for a long time doesn't mean that it's not there.

123 kakapos left in the wild

Kakapo (owl parrot)

Seychelles giant tortoise

Thylacine (Tasmanian tiger)

Mammals

Mammals are some of the most **complex** animals on **Earth**. From the tiny **hog-nosed bat** to the huge BLUE WHALE, mammals have **adapted to every ENVIROMENT** and **habitat**.

What sets **mammals** apart from other **animal groups** is that **they have hair** and **nurse their young with MILK**. The majority of mammals also have **specialized teeth**. Most mammals **give birth to live young**, although two **families** of ancient mammals, the ECHIDNAS and the **platypus**, lay **eggs**. Another group, the **marsupials**, keep their **young** in a **pouch** until they are developed enough to **survive on their own**.

Mammals **under threat**

CR

Western gorilla
Gorillas are the largest members of the ape family. They are under threat from loggers who clear their forest habitat and build roads, which allows hunters in. Poachers kill them for the bushmeat trade. Gorillas are also being wiped out by the deadly Ebola virus.

VU

Bilby
This small, nocturnal, Australian animal is hunted for its silky fur. Many are accidentally killed in rabbit traps and by eating poisoned bait. Introduced cats and foxes also prey on bilbies. Long periods of drought are increasingly putting pressure on bilby populations.

EN

Blue whale
Blue whales are the biggest animals on the planet. They inhabit the open ocean where they feed on tiny krill. Once hunted legally for their meat and oil, they are now protected, but are affected by noise and chemical pollution, and rising sea temperatures.

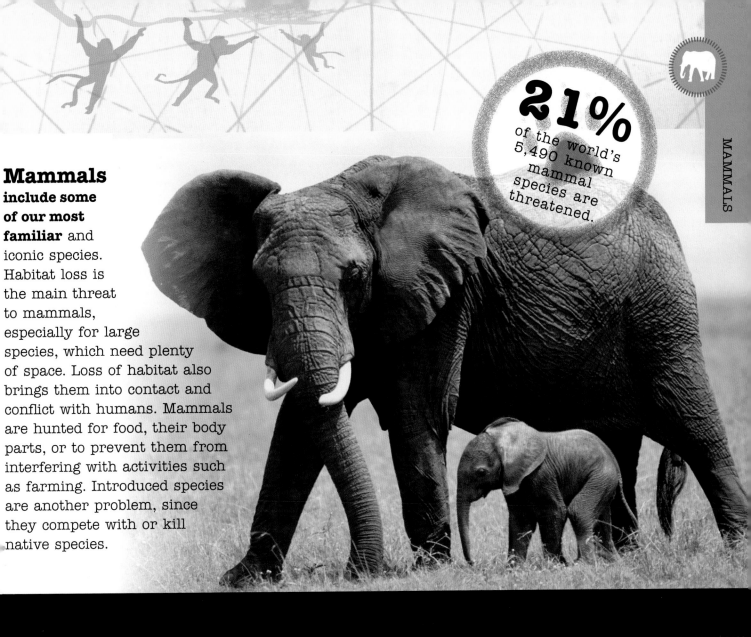

Mammals

include some of our most familiar and iconic species. Habitat loss is the main threat to mammals, especially for large species, which need plenty of space. Loss of habitat also brings them into contact and conflict with humans. Mammals are hunted for food, their body parts, or to prevent them from interfering with activities such as farming. Introduced species are another problem, since they compete with or kill native species.

21% of the world's 5,490 known mammal species are threatened.

EW

Scimitar-horned oryx

Named for its long, curved horns, which are highly prized as hunting trophies, this oryx has been hunted to the brink of extinction. It was also taken for its meat and hides. Climate change is making its habitat increasingly dry and arid. It now survives only in captivity.

VU

Asiatic black bear

Asiatic bears are also known as moon bears because of the crescent marking on their chest. These bears have long been used in traditional local medicines, which is a major cause of their decline. They also face threats from deforestation and human invasion of their habitat.

VU

Giant anteater

These long-nosed creatures excel at vacuuming up large quantities of ants and termites. Both anteaters and their habitat are threatened by land clearance for agricultural use, and by natural and deliberately started bushfires. They are also hunted.

Jaguar

Panthera onca

Jaguars live all over **Central and South America**, mostly in tropical rain forests. But the forests are being cleared and the jaguar is slowly being forced into much smaller areas.

Stealth cat

The jaguar, the largest cat in the Americas, is a fierce predator. It has the strongest jaw of all the cats—suffocating prey by holding on to the throat or piercing the skull with its sharp teeth. Jaguars are ambush predators. They prefer to stalk and ambush their prey rather than chase it. Sometimes they haul the carcass up a tree to eat it.

main threats

- **Habitat loss**—their forest home is being torn apart by humans.
- **Poaching**—although it is illegal, jaguars are hunted for fur and body parts.
- **Conflict with humans**—jaguars are shot by farmers trying to protect their livestock and livelihood.

FACT: Jaguars do most of their hunting at dawn

The jaguar is the third largest cat in the world, after lions and tigers.

Camouflage
The jaguar's coat is perfectly patterned to help it blend into the light and shade of the jungle. Occasionally a jaguar is born with a black coat, but its rosette pattern can still be seen.

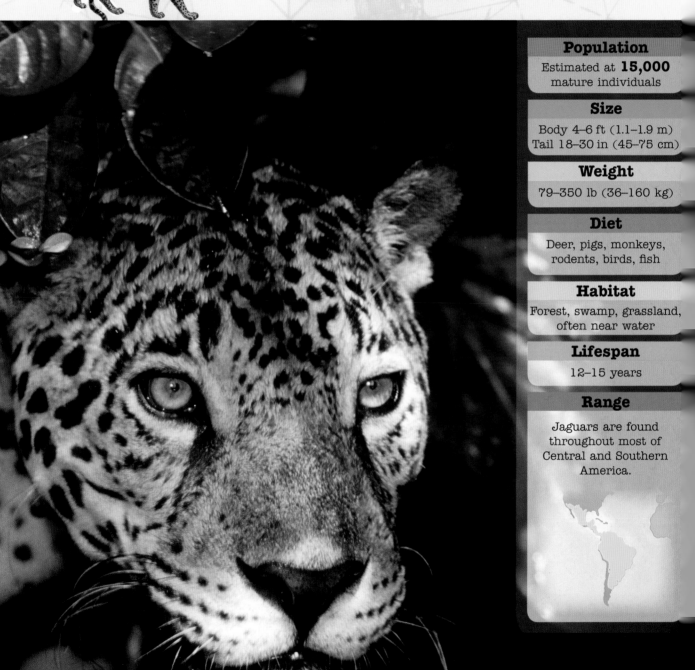

Population
Estimated at **15,000** mature individuals

Size
Body 4–6 ft (1.1–1.9 m)
Tail 18–30 in (45–75 cm)

Weight
79–350 lb (36–160 kg)

Diet
Deer, pigs, monkeys, rodents, birds, fish

Habitat
Forest, swamp, grassland, often near water

Lifespan
12–15 years

Range
Jaguars are found throughout most of Central and Southern America.

and dusk, although they will hunt at other times.

The **BIG** issue: **HABITAT**

Like the jaguar, all the big cats need a large area for their territory. Isolating them in small pockets of forest makes it hard for them to find enough food and a mate. The answer is to connect all the territories with a corridor.

Threat: Land clearance

Large areas of forest are being cleared for agriculture. This land is then used as grazing for cattle or to grow cash crops, such as soya beans or oil palms.

Farm animals are easy prey for jaguars. Big cats sometimes kill horses or adult cattle, although they usually prey on the more vulnerable calves. Farmers kill jaguars to protect their livestock.

Rain forests contain many natural resources, and many people earn money from them. Trees are cut for wood, minerals are dug from the ground, and new roads are built. As the forest is carved up, each jaguar's territory shrinks and it becomes separated from other jaguars. Leaving corridors of forest between the territories allows the animals to move around and find a mate.

Although jaguars can mate and give birth at any time of year, they are more likely to give birth in the wet season, when there is more prey. Between two and four cubs are born at a time.

FACT: Like the other big cats, jaguars roar, but this

Jaguars have been driven out of **40%** of their historical range.

Solution: Jaguar corridor

Jaguar corridors are not only good for jaguars—they also preserve the habitat for other rain forest species. By saving jaguars, conservationists also protect many other animals.

Instead of poaching jaguars and illegally trading in their fur or bones, local people are given alternative employment. Some are training to become guides for groups trekking through the rain forest.

can sound like a very bad cough!

Sumatran orangutan

Pongo abelii

Orangutan translates as "people of the forest." These large apes are rarely found on the ground, preferring a life high up in the treetops.

Orangutans share **96.4%** of our DNA

What a great ape!

A member of the great ape family, orangutans have long, powerful arms for swinging in the trees, and hands and feet that easily grip branches. They are thought to be highly intelligent, since they have been seen making tools for extracting insects and for scratching themselves!

main **threats**

Habitat loss—trees are being cut down, both legally and illegally, to make way for crops, roads, and for the wood trade.

Pet trade—it's illegal to capture orangutans for the pet trade, but poachers are rarely prosecuted, so the trade continues.

Hunting—they are killed as pests when foraging for fruit at the forest edges. Also hunted occasionally for food.

Palm oil plantations
Palm oil is in high demand as a food ingredient and a biofuel, so huge areas of land have been cleared to provide it. This has destroyed much of the orangutans' rain-forest habitat.

FACT: Every evening, high up in the trees, orangutans

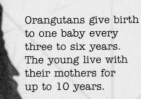

Orangutans give birth to one baby every three to six years. The young live with their mothers for up to 10 years.

Home alone
Females are often killed by hunters out to snatch babies for the pet trade. This leaves the youngsters helpless, since they are totally reliant on their mothers to teach them how to find food, use tools, and make shelters.

Population
Around **7,300**

Size
31–38 in (78–97 cm) head–body length

Weight
88–200 lb (40–90 kg)

Diet
Mainly fruit and seeds, but also bark, leaves, and sometimes insects.

Habitat
Tropical forests

Lifespan
Up to 45 years

Range
There are two species of orangutan. One lives on the Indonesian island of Sumatra, the other lives on Borneo.

Sumatra
Borneo

Back to school
In the wild, orangutans spend over half their day searching for food. When babies are orphaned, sanctuary staff take over the mother's role, teaching the young how to forage and what to eat.

Playtime
Young orangutans often play together, but once they are adults, they live quiet lives in the trees—the females with their young, and the males on their own.

build a brand-new leafy nest to sleep in.

EN # Sea otter
Enhydra lutris

Sea otters rarely come ashore and even sleep in the water. So they don't get swept away by the current, otters wrap themselves in strands of seaweed and float on the tide.

Marine specialist

The sea otter is a strong swimmer and uses its tail like a boat rudder to help it steer through the water. It has the densest fur of any animal, and its thick coat keeps it warm in the icy seas. It has pouches of skin under its arms that can hold food as it swims up from the seabed. Its favorite food is sea urchins.

Population
Up to **107,000** mature individuals

Size
4½–5 ft (1.4–1.5 m)

Weight
72–100 lb (33–45 kg)

Diet
Sea urchins, crabs, mussels

Habitat
Coastal seas

Lifespan
12–15 years

Range
Northern coastal waters stretching from the Kamchatka Peninsula, Russia, to Alaska and California.

Pacific Ocean

Northern sea otter
Russian sea otter
Southern sea otter

main **threats**

 Hunting—otters were once hunted almost to extinction for their fur coats, and populations are still recovering.

 Pollution—oil spills can be disastrous for sea otters.

 Predators—when other prey becomes rare, sea otters move to the top of the menu for killer whales.

  FACT: The sea otter's coat is incredibly thick—it has around

Sea otters are much larger than land otters.

Sea otters control the numbers of sea urchins that graze on the kelp forests. Urchins eat through the base of the kelp strands, which then float away. Without sea otters, the kelp forests would die. The otters are called a keystone species because they are key to the survival of the kelp forest ecosystem.

Otter conservation

Demand for the sea otter's fur led to intensive hunting in the 18th and 19th centuries, reducing populations dramatically in some areas. To help numbers recover, groups of otters are being reintroduced to the seas of North America.

Swimming lessons

Otter pups separated from their mothers can be cared for in captivity and taught how to swim and look after themselves. When they are ready, the sea otters are reintroduced to the wild. It may take several attempts before they can be released.

Rafting sea otters

When resting, sea otters float together in groups called rafts. Usually these rafts involve just a few animals, but sometimes hundreds of otters gather together. Some members of the group will link paws to stop themselves from floating apart.

one million hairs in every square inch of fur.

Ethiopian wolf

Canis simensis

High in the Ethiopian highlands lives a rare species of wolf. Life for the wolf is increasingly difficult as people take over its habitat, bringing with them another hazard—dogs.

Pack life

Ethiopian wolves are sociable animals, living in big family groups called packs. These are made up mostly of adult males and young wolves, with a few adult females. Only one of these, called the "dominant" female, gives birth, but the others help to look after her pups and feed them.

main **threats**

Habitat loss—grasslands are being cleared for crops and grazing land, splitting up wolf populations and reducing the numbers of prey.

Domestic dogs—dogs interbreed with wolves, so there are fewer pure-breed wolves.

Disease—dogs carry diseases such as rabies and distemper, which are easily passed on to the wolf population.

Human impact—wolves are often hit by cars or killed by farmers.

FACT: Wolves don't always eat their prey right away—

Once a year, the dominant female gives birth to between two and six pups. This happens in a hollowed-out den, either in open ground, under rocks, or in a crevice.

Dog danger

Interbreeding and the spread of disease between dogs and wolves are real dangers, so wolves are checked regularly, and dogs are vaccinated against diseases. Local farmers are also encouraged to protect the wolves' habitat.

Hiding out
Small mammals such as hares and grass rats are stalked by the wolves, who hide among cattle herds to avoid detection.

Digging deep
Ethiopian wolves are experts at digging out their main prey, giant mole rats, from their underground burrows.

On patrol
Wolves hunt alone, but meet up with the rest of the pack at dawn and dusk to patrol and scent-mark their territory.

The wolf stalks its victim quietly, crouching low, with its tail down.

Population
Around **500** individuals

Size
44–56 in (110–140 cm) head to tail

Weight
24–44 lb (11–20 kg)

Diet
Mole rats, grass rats, hares, hyraxes. Rarely, young antelopes.

Habitat
Mountain grasslands above 10,000 ft (3,000 m)

Lifespan
11 years in the wild

Range
Seven populations are spread across the Ethiopian highlands at 10,000–15,000 ft (3,000–4,500 m).

they often kill it, then hide it to eat later.

MAMMALS

Manatee

Trichechus—three species

Also known as sea cows, manatees are the gentle grazers of the oceans. They feed on the sea grasses that grow in the shallow coastal waters of the tropics.

Sailors used to think manatees were mermaids.

Mistaken for mermaids

The manatee and its close relative, the dugong, are large, slow-moving sea mammals. They swim and glide using their short, paddlelike flippers and large tails. The manatee's peglike teeth are constantly worn away by its tough plant diet and replaced with new teeth.

main **threats**

- **Collisions with boats**—many get hit by motor boats or caught up in the boat's propellers because they can't hear them.

- **Coastal development**—changes of land use threaten their feeding grounds.

- **Hunting**—they are hunted for their meat and hides, despite being protected.

- **Poisoning**—blooms of toxic algae produce a nerve poison that affects the brain of manatees and dugongs.

Population
Fewer than **10,000** of each species

Size
12–15 ft
(3.7–4.6 m)

Weight
Average: 1,750–2,650 lb
(800–1,200 kg)

Diet
Sea grasses and other plants and algae

Habitat
Coastal waters, estuaries, rivers

Lifespan
More than 50 years

Range
There are three species of manatee. These are the West Indian manatee, the West African manatee, and the Amazonian manatee. The Amazonian is the only one that lives solely in fresh water.

West Indian manatee

Amazonian manatee

West African manatee

FACT: West Indian manatees relax by lying on

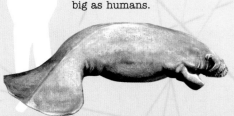

Adult manatees are more than twice as big as humans.

Saving manatees

The biggest threat to the West Indian manatee is from motor boats. In some places, the boats are restricted or even banned. Scientists are also designing guards for propellers and trying to adjust engines so that manatees can hear them.

Manatees can't see very well. They explore their surroundings by touch, using their bristly muzzles and muscular lips.

Dugong

Manatee

Manatee or dugong?

There is an easy way to tell manatees and dugongs apart—manatees have a large paddle-shaped tail, while dugongs have a fluke like a whale.

their backs on the seabed.

EN Tasmanian devil

Sarcophilus harrisii

If you live in Tasmania, you may hear an eerie screeching late at night. This is the sound of a Tasmanian devil, a bad-tempered but feisty little marsupial.

Devil in detail

Tasmanian devils are short, stocky, bearlike animals about the size of a small dog. They have a coat of coarse brown or black fur, and often have white markings on their chests and sides. Their powerful jaws are filled with sharp teeth that can crack bones. Although they are solitary animals, they will gather in groups to feed on a large carcass.

Facing disaster

Devils are under threat from a deadly disease. No one knows how it spreads, but it may be passed on when devils bite each other. Large painful lumps form around the devil's mouth and it slowly starves to death. Scientists are trying to protect disease-free populations and are breeding devils in captivity to increase numbers.

main **threats**

- ✚ **Disease**—a fatal, infectious face disease is wiping them out at an alarming rate.
- 🐾 **Competition**—red foxes are taking over the devil's territory as the devil's population goes down.
- ◎ **Hunting**—early settlers trapped and poisoned thousands of devils until they were made a protected species in 1941.

FACT: The ears of Tasmanian devils turn

Baby devils grow in a pouch on their mother's stomach. Females give birth to as many as 30 young at a time, but only three or four survive.

Foxy foe

Introduced red foxes and devils share the same habitat, so if the devils are wiped out, the foxes are likely to take over and may eliminate many native species.

Population

Up to **25,000** mature individuals

Size

25 in (64 cm) head-to-body length

Weight

15–26 lb (7–12 kg)

Diet

Prefers to eat dead animals, but will also prey on snakes, insects, birds, and small animals up to the size of a wombat.

Habitat

Coastal shrublands and forests

Lifespan

Up to 6 years

Range

Tasmanian devils once lived all over Australia, but are now found only on the island of Tasmania.

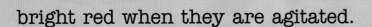

bright red when they are agitated.

VU

Polar bear

Ursus maritimus

Imagine if the ground you walked on suddenly started to disappear. This is the problem facing the world's largest land carnivore, the polar bear, as the Arctic sea ice melts.

King of the north

These enormous bears are well adapted for living on snow and ice with thick fur and a layer of body fat for warmth. Their broad feet spread their weight on thin ice and have rough pads that prevent them from slipping.

main **threats**

Climate change—rapid and widespread melting of sea ice in summer means bears have to swim farther to find food.

Food supply—melting of sea ice forces seals to migrate. The bears must rely on their fat reserves until the ice refreezes and they can hunt seals again.

Hunting—hunting for their meat and skin takes place even though it is illegal.

Pollution—chemicals build up in seal fat and are passed on to the bears, affecting their health. Oil spills reduce the insulation of the bears' fur, so they can freeze to death.

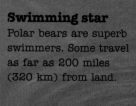

Swimming star
Polar bears are superb swimmers. Some travel as far as 200 miles (320 km) from land.

Adult bears are mostly solitary, although males may group together during the open-water season in summer and fall.

FACT: Under their white fur, polar bears have black skin,

Male bears can be a massive 10 ft (3 m) long.

Hungry bears

Polar bears need sea ice to get to their food and travel between their hunting grounds and dens. If they become stranded on land they can starve. Bears have been known to wander into towns to find food, which brings them into conflict with humans.

Seal hunting

Polar bears stalk seals, lying in wait for them beside air holes in the ice. As the seals surface, they are swiped with a mighty forepaw, grabbed by the neck, and dragged out. Polar bears also hunt seals under the ice, and also on land, digging seal pups out of the snow caves where they were born.

Population
20,000–25,000

Size
Males 8–10 ft (2.5–3 m)
Females are smaller

Weight
450–1,300 lb
(200–600 kg)

Diet
Mainly seals, also beluga whales, walrus, mammals, waterfowl

Habitat
Sea ice and snowy coastal areas

Lifespan
Up to 20 years in the wild

Range
Arctic Circle

Birthing caves

In the winter, females dig a snow cave in which they hibernate and give birth. The mother and cubs stay hidden there until the spring. Cubs live with their mother for two to three years.

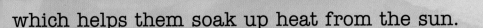

which helps them soak up heat from the sun.

Black **rhinoceros**

Diceros bicornis

These hefty vegetarians have a reputation for aggression, charging at anything that gets in their way. They like their space and snort, honk, and roar to warn others away.

Mega herbivore

Rhinos have short, stocky legs to hold up their enormous bulk. They have leathery, virtually hairless skin and two large horns (made of keratin) on their snouts. Their vision is poor, but they make up for it with their keen senses of hearing and smell. They forage in the cool dusk and dawn and rest during the day.

main **threats**

- **Hunting**—rhinos are poached for their horns, which are used in traditional oriental medicine and for dagger handles.
- **Habitat loss**—land cleared for settlement and growing crops has resulted in fewer suitable habitats.
- **Civil unrest**—war and civil unrest in various African countries has hindered conservation efforts.

Population
Around **4,180** across three subspecies

Size
Up to 10 ft (3 m) head-to-tail length

Weight
1–1.4 tons (900–1,300 kg)

Diet
Woody plants, stoft-stemmed plants, and grasses

Habitat
Mainly grassy plains, but also deserts and dry woodland

Lifespan
Up to 40 years

Range
Three subspecies of black rhinoceros live in southern and eastern Africa. A fourth subspecies, native to Cameroon, is thought to be extinct.

FACT: Black rhinos have a hooklike, grasping top lip that helps

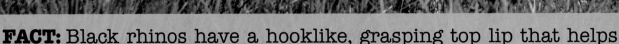

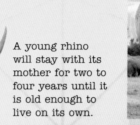

A young rhino will stay with its mother for two to four years until it is old enough to live on its own.

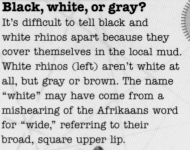

Black, white, or gray?
It's difficult to tell black and white rhinos apart because they cover themselves in the local mud. White rhinos (left) aren't white at all, but gray or brown. The name "white" may have come from a mishearing of the Afrikaans word for "wide," referring to their broad, square upper lip.

Poaching
Selling rhino horn is illegal, but the horns fetch high prices so the poaching continues. Some rhinos have their horns removed in the hope that this will stop the killing.

Bodyguards
Rhinos of all species are now heavily protected within special conservation areas. These are patrolled day and night by armed rangers to try and deter poachers.

them to grab woody branches and rip up leaves.

Birds

Feathers are what make **BIRDS** the **masters of the air** and distinct from other animal groups. There are around **10,000 species** that **vary in size** from the tiniest of **hummingbirds** to the **enormous ostrich**.

Although all birds have wings, not all of them can **fly**. Birds also have a **BEAK**, a **lightweight skeleton**, scaly legs, and lay **eggs** with hard shells. Some are adapted to **swimming** and have **webbed feet**. Many live in large flocks, while others live on their own or in **small family groups**.

Birds **under threat**

Bali starling

This starling's striking coloring has pushed it to the edge of extinction because of demand from the pet trade. Habitat loss and competition for nest sites with the black-winged starling are also affecting the bird's survival.

Indian vulture

Populations of this once-common bird have plummeted since the mid-1990s. The cause is known to be a drug given to herds of cattle and goats that causes kidney failure in the vultures when they scavenge carcasses. Safer drugs are now being used to treat sick livestock.

Black stilt

Only 85 adult black stilts are thought to exist in the wild. These wading birds nest on a river that has been affected by upstream dams that have changed the habitat through drainage and flooding. The birds are also under attack from native and introduced predators.

Birds are facing a number of threats.

Habitat loss and climate change are expected to have a huge impact on bird populations. Brightly colored birds are regularly hunted for their feathers or for the pet trade. Songbirds also make popular pets, and in some countries they are trapped and eaten as delicacies. Introduced species eat eggs and chicks, or compete for nesting sites. Overfishing is another serious problem, since it deprives seabirds of food. They also get trapped or injured in fishing gear.

There are thought to be 190 bird species that are critically endangered. The biggest threat they face is from agriculture, which clears trees and bushes used for nesting and changes the types of food available for the birds to eat.

EN

Hyacinth macaw
The hyacinth macaw is the largest member of the parrot family. Its attractive plumage has made it popular as a pet. Macaws are losing habitat through land clearance and illegal logging.

EN

Asian crested ibis
The striking crest of this bird has been its downfall. Once hunted almost to extinction for its feathers, the crested ibis has been saved by a captive breeding program. Habitat loss and degradation have reduced its natural range across northern Asia to one remaining stronghold in China.

VU

Malleefowl
Malleefowl are ground-dwelling birds that lay their eggs in a mound of warm sand and leave them to hatch. Climate change may be the reason why chicks are failing to hatch, and bushfires and predation by introduced foxes may be behind the general drop in numbers.

EN

Yellow-eyed penguin
These are thought to be the rarest penguins in the world. The cutting down of forests along coastlines is forcing them to nest in more open dune areas where adults, eggs, and chicks fall prey to introduced species such as cats, stoats, and rats.

VU Southern **rockhopper**

Eudyptes chrysocome

Both species of rockhopper penguin—southern and northern—are declining in number, but no one knows why. Possible causes are climate change and too much fishing.

Punk rockhoppers

These small, red-eyed, reddish-brown-billed penguins are famous for their funky-looking yellow eyebrow feathers. They get their name from the way they hop from rock to rock on their Southern Ocean island homes. They are incredibly noisy, using loud shrieks to defend their territory, scare off predators, and attract mates.

Rookeries

Rockhoppers live in nesting pairs—there are thousands in each breeding colony. The females lay two eggs, but usually only one hatches. The male looks after the newborn chick, while the female hunts. Older chicks huddle in groups when both parents go fishing.

main **threats**

- **Food supply**—heavy fishing for squid may be reducing food supplies, leading to starvation.

- **Predators**—subantarctic fur seals are hunting penguins as food and competing with them for fish.

- **Climate change**—rising sea temperatures appear to be reducing the numbers of krill and other prey.

FACT: You can tell which species is which by their eyebrows—

While the female rockhopper is away hunting, the male vomits up "milk" from his stomach to feed the chick.

Where's the food gone?
All penguin species are having problems finding enough food. Rising sea temperatures and unpredictable climate changes are forcing prey to move to new areas and penguins have to travel farther to find it. Humans are also taking too many fish, which means there is less for penguins to eat.

Population
Several hundred thousand remain, but some populations have halved in size.

Size
20 in (52 cm) tall

Weight
6½ lb (3 kg)

Diet
Mainly krill, also squid, crustaceans, octopus, fish

Habitat
Nests on cliffs and rocky gullies on ocean islands, near fresh water

Lifespan
Around 10 years

Range
The southern rockhopper and northern rockhopper live on different islands in the Southern Ocean.

Northern rockhopper (*Eudyptes moseleyi*)
Southern rockhopper (*Eudyptes chrysocome*)

Southern rockhoppers are classed as vulnerable because their numbers have dropped rapidly in recent years. The northern rockhopper, however, is classed as endangered. Some populations of northern rockhoppers have gone down by 90 percent in the last 50 years.

the northern birds definitely win on length!

Whooping crane

Grus americana

The whooping crane is a very special bird. Once, it was almost wiped out, but it's gradually making a comeback on the plains of North America.

Crane on the plain

Early settlers drove the whooping crane from its wetland nesting grounds and shot it for meat, so by 1941 only 16 were left in northwest Canada. Since then, a breeding program has saved the crane from extinction. The only problem is, the eggs are taken away from their parents to be hatched, so breeders have to teach the babies how to do everything, from finding food to flying south for the winter.

Population
550+ birds in the wild and captivity

Size
5 ft (1.5 m) tall, wingspan 7½ ft (2.3 m)

Weight
13½–17 lb (6–7 kg)

Diet
Frogs, rodents, snails, fish, insects, berries, grain

Habitat
Marsh areas, prairie, shallow lakes

Lifespan
30+ years in the wild

Range
One original nesting site in Alberta, Canada; a breeding site in Wisconsin; and two overwintering sites in the South.

Alberta site

Wisconsin site

■ Nesting site
□ Overwintering site

main **threats**

Habitat loss—their original breeding sites in the north have been taken over for farming, and the southern wetlands where they overwinter have been drained.

Predators—nestlings are prey for wolves, black bears, wolverines, foxes, golden eagles, and lynx.

FACT: Whoopers, as the birds are called locally, get their

Whooping cranes are the tallest birds in North America. They stand almost as tall as a person.

Cranes have a patch of red skin on their head, a black "mustache," yellow eyes, and a long, pointed bill.

Long-legged wader
Adult cranes have long dark legs and snowy white bodies, while the fledglings (babies) have brown feathers that change to white as the chick grows. Whooping cranes lay between one and three eggs, but usually only one survives. They build their nests out of bulrushes and other wetland plants in shallow water. The male bird protects the nest against danger.

name from the loud whooping call they make.

The **BIG** issue: **MIGRATION**

How do you teach a bird to migrate when it has no idea where to go? Get it to follow an ultralight aircraft of course!

Problem: How to be a crane

Bringing up baby

As part of their conservation program, breeders hatch crane eggs in incubators. To prevent the chicks thinking humans are their parents, handlers wear costumes and use hand puppets when they teach them how to feed and behave.

Reach for the skies

Some birds instinctively know their migration route, but cranes need to be shown the way. Breeders play ultralight-engine sounds while the chicks are still in the egg. Once they have their flight feathers, they're trained to follow the ultralight and taken for short trips.

FACT: Fossils of whooping cranes dating back several million

Solution: Flight training

Flying south for the winter

In the autumn, breeders ring the young birds and take them on their 1,900 km (1,200 mile) journey from the breeding centre in Wisconsin to Florida. Along the way, they rest in suitable feeding grounds. Once they arrive, they're left to fend for themselves and find their own way back in the spring. After that, they can migrate every year without help.

Power lines are one of the biggest threats to new fledglings, so in some areas there are special power-line markers. These are fluorescent, multi-colored, plastic plates designed specially for birds' vision. They hang from the lines, turn in the wind, and glow at night for up to 10 hours.

The pilot of the ultralight has to wear his costume all the way to Florida!

Reptiles

Reptiles have walked on **EARTH** for **320 million years.** There are nearly **9,000 different** species, which include **lizards**, **snakes**, turtles, **tuataras**, and crocodiles.

Reptiles have a **BACKBONE** and most have **four legs,** but some are legless. They are **cold-blooded** and need **warmth from the sun** to keep **ACTIVE**. Most species **lay eggs**, although some **give BIRTH to live young**. All reptiles have a **SCALY SKIN** that prevents them from **drying out**.

Reptiles **under threat**

CR

VU

VU

Gharial
This slender-snouted crocodilian gets its name from the lump at the end of the male's nose, which looks like an Indian pot called a ghara. Changes in river use have had a huge impact on the gharial's habitat. Gharials are also killed by fishermen, who compete for fish stocks.

King cobra
This venomous snake is found across Southeast Asia. When confronted, it flares its hood and hisses aggressively. It is threatened by loss of its forest habitat and collection of adult snakes for the pet, skin, food, and medicine trades.

Brothers Island tuatara
Tuataras are the last surviving link to an ancient group of reptiles that evolved 200 million years ago. Only two species remain. Although tuataras can live up to 100 years, they are slow to breed. They are under threat from introduced species and climate change.

Reptiles play a key role in many ecosystems.

If they disappear, many other species will be affected. Among the many threats reptiles face are habitat loss, climate change, pollution, invasive species, and disease. They are also hunted for food and the pet trade.

Stormy weather

Scientists think reptiles may be even more vulnerable to climate change than amphibians. They estimate that 20% of reptile species could vanish as a result of changing weather patterns over the next 70 years.

28% of the world's reptiles are threatened.

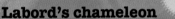

VU

Labord's chameleon

Labord's chameleon is an unusual lizard because it lives for only one year and spends up to seven months of that time as an egg. Habitat degradation is making it vulnerable to extinction.

CR

EW

VU

Chinese three-striped box turtle

Some people believe that eating the meat of this turtle will cure them of cancer, which is why the species has almost been wiped out in the wild. It is also highly sought after for the pet trade because of its bright coloring.

Pinta Island tortoise

Only one example of this giant tortoise, nicknamed "Lonesome George," now exists. The other 10 species of Galápagos tortoise have been reduced in numbers because people and introduced species hunt them for food. Goats and cattle also compete with them for vegetation.

Marine iguana

Marine iguanas are the only lizards that swim in the sea and feed on seaweed. Oil spills and pollution are destroying their food sources and nesting beaches, and introduced cats, dogs, and rats are eating the iguanas and their eggs.

Leatherback turtle

Dermochelys coriacea

Leatherbacks are the largest of all sea turtles. Powered by their huge front flippers, these turtles crisscross the oceans, traveling thousands of miles every year.

Shell, what shell?

Unlike other turtles, the leatherback doesn't have a hard shell. Instead, it has thick, ridged, oily skin with bony plates underneath. Leatherbacks can dive much deeper than other turtles. Some have been known to go as deep as 4,200 ft (1,300 m). Leatherbacks have hard, horny points on their upper jaws instead of teeth, and backward-pointing spines in their throats to help them swallow food.

Yummy jellyfish
Leatherbacks are the main predators of jellyfish. Jellyfish eat young finfish and larvae, so without leatherbacks to keep the jellyfish under control, many important fish stocks could be affected.

FACT: Every female leatherback has a unique pink mark on

An average turtle's front flippers can be as long as 9 ft (2.7 m)!

Turtle conservation

In some countries, fishing nets have to include a special trapdoor that lets turtles escape. The beaches where they lay their eggs are being protected from developers and natural erosion, and the authorities are also clamping down on illegal egg collection.

main **threats**

- ⊕ **Hunting**—leatherbacks are hunted sometimes for their meat, but mostly for their eggs. They also get caught in fishing nets or on longline hooks, and drown.
- **Pollution**—turtles mistake plastic bags, balloons, and other plastic waste for jellyfish.
- **Habitat**—many nesting beaches are being destroyed by development along the coast.

Population
Uncertain, but known to be declining rapidly in the Pacific

Size
3¼–6½ ft (1–2 m)

Weight
550–1,500 lb (250–700 kg)

Diet
Jellyfish, sea squirts

Habitat
Open seas

Lifespan
Possibly 20–30 years

Range
Throughout the world's oceans, except the coldest areas of the Arctic and Antarctic. Nests only on tropical beaches.

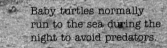

Baby turtles normally run to the sea during the night to avoid predators.

One moonless night
Female leatherbacks come ashore every two or three years to lay their eggs in the warm sand of tropical beaches. They often return to the same beach where they were born.

Male or female?
After digging a hole, the female lays up to 110 eggs, covering them with sand to hide them from predators. High temperatures inside the nest produce females; low ones produce males.

Heading back out
Around 60 days later, the hatchlings emerge under cover of darkness and make their way down to the sea. Male leatherback turtles never return to land again.

the top of her head that can be used for identification.

VU **Komodo** dragon

Varanus komodoensis

Do dragons really exist? Maybe not, but on five small islands in Indonesia there are meat-eating monster lizards that have a bite that can kill.

Dangerous dragons

Komodo dragons are the largest lizards in the world. They have a long body, short, sturdy legs, a thick, muscular tail, and a forked yellow tongue. Their powerful jaws can tear animal carcasses apart and deliver a poisonous bite to live prey. Their saliva also carries deadly bacteria that infects the wound and leads to blood poisoning. The dragon follows its victim for several days until it dies from loss of blood.

Agile hunters

Komodo dragons are good swimmers and hunt in the surf for fish and seabirds. Young dragons can climb trees to escape predators, including adult dragons.

FACT: Komodo dragons can outrun a person, reaching speeds

Looking after dragons
Komodo dragons have been protected since the 1930s within the Komodo National Park. They are a tourist attraction, which provides money for local people, encouraging them to look after the dragons. Conservationists are trying to breed dragons in captivity, and stop poaching and loss of the dragon's habitat outside the park.

main **threats**

🎯 **Hunting**—dragons are prime targets for big-game hunters. They are also killed for their skin and feet to make novelties.

🚜 **Habitat loss**—forests are being cleared by farmers to grow crops. Poachers start forest fires, which also reduces habitat.

🍴 **Food supply**—poaching is reducing the rusa deer, the dragon's main prey.

🔥 **Natural hazards**—volcanic eruptions, earthquakes, and wildfires have all affected dragon populations.

Population
Around **3,000**

Size
Up to 10 ft (3 m) long

Weight
More than 150 lb (70 kg)

Diet
Mainly carrion, but also live deer, wild pigs, birds, goats, reptiles

Habitat
Hot, dry grasslands and tropical forest

Lifespan
Up to 50 years in the wild

Range
Indonesian islands: Lesser Sunda Islands of Rinca, Komodo, Flores, Gili Montang, and Gili Dasami.

◻ Current populations

Follow that smell!
Dragons smell with their tongues. They use it to find dead animals up to 6 miles (10 km) away. If lots of dragons arrive at the same carcass, the largest and most dominant dragons eat first. Sometimes they wrestle with each other and the loser is killed and eaten.

of 11 mph (18 kph) over short distances on land.

Amphibians

Amphibians are a group of **vertebrate animals** that include **frogs**, **toads**, salamanders, caecilians, and **newts**.

THERE ARE MORE than **6,700 known species of amphibian**. **They are the descendants** of the first animals to leave the water and walk on land— **400 MILLION** YEARS AGO.

Amphibians are found on **EVERY CONTINENT** except **Antarctica**. The greatest number **of species is found in RAIN FORESTS**, where they **thrive** in the **damp atmosphere**. Amphibians take in some of their **oxygen** through their **SKIN**, which needs to be kept moist. **Most species also need to lay their eggs in fresh water.**

Amphibians under threat

CR

Giant Chinese salamander
This is the world's largest amphibian, growing up to 5 ft (1.5 m) in length. It is fully aquatic and lives in cold, fast-running streams. Considered a delicacy, it is under threat from hunting, the building of dams, and pollution.

EW

Kihansi spray toad
This species lived only on the wet rocks in the spray zone of the Kihansi Falls in Tanzania. Dam construction cut off most of its water supply, and the number of toads plummeted. The species is now kept alive through captive breeding, but it is hoped that some can be returned to the wild.

VU

Darwin's frog
Darwin's frog has an unusual pointed snout and a triangular head. The male uses his vocal sac to brood the tadpoles until they turn into baby frogs. Deforestation and drought have led to a sharp decline in the numbers of these frogs.

Scientists use amphibians as an indicator of the health of an ecosystem.

They are so sensitive to changes in climate, habitat, and pollution that if their numbers decrease rapidly, there must be something wrong. Since the 1970s, amphibian numbers have plummeted.

32% of amphibian species are facing extinction.

Fatal fungus

One of the biggest threats currently facing amphibians is the deadly disease chytridiomycosis. It is caused by a fungus that attacks the skin, leading to problems with the animal's breathing and water uptake. The fungus has spread around the world, killing local populations of amphibians, and sometimes every last member of the species.

Corroboree frog

Found in mountain woodland in a small area of Australia, this tiny, poisonous frog is suffering the effects of climate change and human encroachment into its breeding grounds. The frogs are also being wiped out by bushfires in summer that destroy their forest environment.

Axolotl

The axolotl is the Peter Pan of the amphibian world—it never grows up. Instead, it stays stuck in its juvenile phase, complete with feathery gills around its head. This salamander lives in a small area of canals and wetlands near Mexico City that is rapidly shrinking.

Goliath frog

Goliath frogs are the largest frogs in the world and grow to be as big as a dinner plate. This makes them ideal for eating, and is the main threat to this species. Their habitat is under threat from deforestation and damming of rivers. They are also popular as pets.

Golden toad

Incilius periglenes

The golden toad once lived high in the thick cloud forests of Costa Rica. It has not been seen there since 1989, and is now thought to be extinct.

Toad gatherings

Not a lot is known about golden toads. These secretive animals may have spent part of their lives hidden in burrows beneath the forest floor, but they gathered in huge numbers during the short breeding season. With eight males to every female, there was fierce competition for mates.

FACT: Only the male toad was the distinctive golden color;

Head in the clouds

The high-altitude forests of Monteverde are frequently blanketed with clouds and mists. They support unique ecosystems and are one of the world's most important wildlife refuges.

Population

No known individuals. Believed to be extinct.

Size

1½—2¼ in (3.9—5.6 cm)

Weight

Unknown

Diet

Probably small invertebrates

Habitat

High-altitude cloud forests

Lifespan

Unknown

Range

Once lived in an area of the Monteverde cloud forest in the north of Costa Rica.

Costa Rica

Monteverde

The mystery of the disappearing toads

Of the 50 species of frog and toad once found in the Monteverde Cloud Forest Reserve, almost half disappeared after suffering huge population crashes in 1987. The cause of these disappearances was mysterious because the remote reserve was protected from human interference. Many ideas have been put forward, but recent research suggests that a combination of factors may have been involved.

main **threats**

- **Climate change**—the El Niño weather event caused a severe dry season in 1987. There were far fewer breeding pools and they dried up more quickly.
- **Disease**—the warmer temperatures created the right conditions for the spread of a deadly fungal skin disease called chytridiomycosis.
- **Habitat**—the golden toads were vulnerable to changes in their environment because they lived in such a small area—only 11 sq. mile (30 sq. km).

the females were darker, with yellow-edged red blotches.

Fish

Fish are **Earth's** EXPERT **SWIMMERS.** Born for a **life in water**, most have a **streamlined body** with SCALES, **fins,** and a **tail for power** and STEERING. **Instead of lungs,** they have **gills** that filter **oxygen** from the water as they swim, so they can **breathe under water.**

Fish were the first animals with a BACKBONE to appear on **Earth,** and are also the **largest group of vertebrate animals— more than 31,000 known species live in water all over the planet.** Most live either in OCEANS or in **freshwater** (lakes, rivers, swamps), but a few **species live in both.**

Fish under threat

Scalloped hammerhead
Hammerheads are among several shark species that are victims of shark-finning—cutting the fins off live sharks. The shark is dropped back into the water, but, unable to swim properly, it drowns or starves to death.

Spotted handfish
The "hands" on a spotted handfish are paired fins that it uses to "walk" along the seabed. It can be found only in one river estuary in Tasmania, Australia. It's thought that the northern Pacific sea star (a kind of starfish) eats handfish eggs and is keeping the population low.

Dusky grouper
This huge fish uses its large bottom jaw to scoop up other fish. Dusky groupers live in shallow water and are easy to see and catch. They have been overfished for food and for sport, and because they breed late in life, their populations are not recovering.

26% of the world's fish species are under threat.

There are four main threats to fish.

Overfishing clears populations of fish faster than they can recover, as well as killing other fish that get caught up in nets. Pollution can have a devastating effect, whether from spills of oil or chemicals, or the dumping of plastics and other garbage. Climate change is raising ocean temperatures—even a few degrees warmer is too hot for some marine life to survive. Freshwater sources are also shrinking, as rivers are dammed and lakes are drained for agriculture.

CR

Beluga sturgeon

These monster fish can grow up to 16½ ft (5 m) in length and take a long time to reach maturity. They are threatened by overfishing for their eggs (caviar), which are considered to be a delicacy, and by the damming of freshwater rivers, blocking access to their spawning sites.

NT

Leafy seadragon

With a body that looks like it is made up of plant fronds, the leafy seadragon is hard to spot among the seaweed. It lives in the coastal waters off Australia among coral reefs and sea grass meadows, but both habitats are shrinking because of pollution from human habitation.

EN

Banggai cardinalfish

The Banggai cardinalfish is found only around the Banggai Islands in eastern Indonesia. This small geographic range and population make it vulnerable to demand from the pet trade, especially tropical fish enthusiasts, who buy it for its striking appearance.

Southern **bluefin tuna**

Thunnus maccoyii

Tuna is one of the tastiest fish in the sea. The bluefin tuna is particularly prized, but demand for its flesh is pushing it to the brink of disaster.

FISH

Population
Believed to have declined by more than **95 percent** since the 1960s

Size
6½–13 ft (2–4 m)

Weight
440–880 lb (200–400 kg)

Diet
Smaller fish, octopus, squid, eels, crustaceans

Lifespan
15–40 years

Range
The southern bluefin lives in the Atlantic, Pacific, and Southern oceans. They are sometimes described as Atlantic or Pacific tunas.

Southern bluefin tuna

Super-fast swimmer

The enormous southern bluefin tuna is one of two species—the other is the northern bluefin, which is also in danger from overfishing. Unusually for fish, bluefins are warm-blooded, which lets them roam great distances through cold water. They are well adapted to speedy swimming, with their stiff, muscular, torpedo-shaped body; powerful tail; and retractable side fins. They are capable of swimming up to an amazing 43 mph (70 kph).

The coloring of tuna—steely blue on top, and silvery white below—provides the perfect camouflage against predators above and below them.

main **threats**

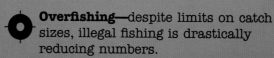

Overfishing—despite limits on catch sizes, illegal fishing is drastically reducing numbers.

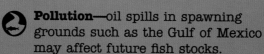

Pollution—oil spills in spawning grounds such as the Gulf of Mexico may affect future fish stocks.

Fact: Thousands of seabirds, turtles, dolphins, and sharks are

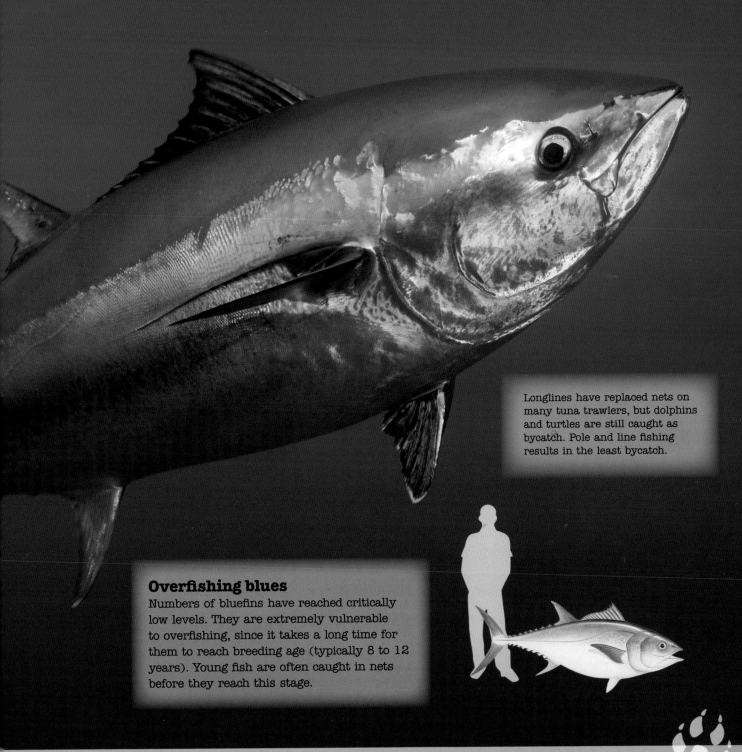

Plight of the albatross
Albatrosses spend much of their life flying over the oceans, but despite their lack of contact with people, many species are under threat from longline tuna fishing. The birds often get hooked as they try to grab bait, and are then dragged under the waves and drowned. Even with net fishing, the birds fly into the cables or become entangled in the nets as they are lifted in.

Longlines have replaced nets on many tuna trawlers, but dolphins and turtles are still caught as bycatch. Pole and line fishing results in the least bycatch.

Overfishing blues
Numbers of bluefins have reached critically low levels. They are extremely vulnerable to overfishing, since it takes a long time for them to reach breeding age (typically 8 to 12 years). Young fish are often caught in nets before they reach this stage.

killed each year as a result of tuna fishing.

Invertebrates

Around **97 percent** of **animal species** are **invertebrates**. This group covers a wide variety of animal types, including **insects, CORALS, worms,** crustaceans, and **spiders.**

DESPITE the fact they are **all so different**, what they do have in common is that they don't have **a backbone**, a BONY SKELETON, or **proper jaws**. Some have a hard outer covering called an **exoskeleton** and others have a **protective shell**. They have adapted to live in a **wide range of habitats,** from **icy water** to SCORCHING DESERTS.

Invertebrates **under threat**

CR

Dracula ant

Dracula ants are named for their habit of feeding on the blood of their larvae. Although this doesn't kill the young, they have been seen trying to escape when adult workers arrive in the chamber. Loss of their tiny forest habitat in Madagascar is putting them under pressure.

EX

Polynesian tree snail

These tiny snails were the unintended victims of an attempt to control African land snails, which had been introduced to the islands. The African snails escaped into the wild and a predatory snail was brought in to control them, but preferred to eat the native tree snails instead.

NT

Horseshoe crab

Horseshoe crabs evolved more than 300 million years ago. Their eggs provide food for millions of seabirds, but development of beaches is affecting their laying sites. Horseshoe crabs play a vital part in human medicine, especially research into vision.

Invertebrates galore

More than 1.3 million species of invertebrate are already known, but millions more remain to be discovered. Although many seem small and unimportant to us, invertebrates are vital to the survival of much bigger species.

Invertebrates face every type of threat to their survival.

Edible species, such as crabs and lobsters, are being overfished and poisoned by pollution. Land-based species are suffering habitat loss, competition from introduced species, extermination as pests, and the effects of climate change.

31%
of invertebrates assessed by IUCN are under threat.

CR

elvet worm

These segmented creatures are not true worms. They have eyes, antennae, and multiple pairs of stub feet with retractable claws. Their unusual behavior of ejecting slime to trap their prey has made them highly collectible for the pet trade, but their main threat is habitat loss.

CR

Shasta crayfish

This freshwater crayfish is found only in the Pit River in California. The building of dams and other habitat changes have split the population into small groups and prevented migration between them. Invasive species are also competing for space and food.

VU

Great raft spider

These spiders are semiaquatic and live near still and slow-moving water. They can run across the surface and hunt for prey under water. The drainage of wetlands and water pollution are damaging their habitat and making them vulnerable to extinction.

Coral reef

Coral reefs are among the richest and most diverse ecosystems on Earth. Although they cover less than one percent of Earth's surface, they are home to 25 percent of all underwater life.

The work of centuries

Reefs are made from the rocky remains of tiny marine animals called polyps that live together in warm, shallow seas. They have a mouth fringed with stinging tentacles and a tubelike body, around which they create a stony cup. Each circle in the picture is the mouth of one polyp.

Coral reefs take thousands of years to build, but up to 70 percent could be wiped out in just a few decades by climate change, pollution, mining for building materials, and harmful fishing practices.

Stressed out

Algae called zooxanthellae live inside some corals, providing nutrients and giving the coral its color. If the corals become stressed, for example, by pollution or rising sea temperatures, the algae are ejected or lose their color. If the stress continues, the corals die. This is called bleaching, because of the white limestone skeletons left behind.

FACT: If a coral reef is not too badly damaged by

Death and destruction

Reefs are prime targets for fishing. Tropical fish for aquariums are stunned using poisonous cyanide, which kills coral. Explosives used to kill shoals of fish also shatter the reef. The coral itself is collected for aquariums and to make jewelry and decorative items.

Reef-dwellers

The nooks and crannies of reefs make ideal homes and hiding places for anemones, shrimp, fish, turtles, sponges, starfish, sea snakes, and crabs. Reefs also attract seabirds and predatory fish, including sharks and groupers.

Brain coral

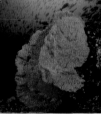

Fan coral

Antler coral

Weird and wonderful

There are around 1,000 different coral species that form colonies in a wide variety of shapes and sizes. Some look like human brains, while others resemble stag's horns, fans, tables, and pillars.

bleaching, it can recover, but this can take up to 10 years.

Monarch butterfly
Danaus plexippus

Monarchs are striking butterflies, with bright orange wings and thick black veins. Every fall, North American monarchs fly thousands of miles south in search of food and warmth. But the butterflies that return home the following spring are not the ones that originally set out.

Migrating monarchs

Monarch butterflies are found in various places around the world, chiefly the Americas, India, and countries around Australia. The usual lifespan of a monarch is two months, but East-coast American butterflies born just before migration are able to live for seven months. This is just long enough to enable them to fly to Mexico, overwinter, lay eggs, and begin the return journey.

Homing in

A big mystery in the monarchs' migration is how the butterflies return to the same trees to overwinter every year. Millions of them roost together, blanketing the branches. There are so many that sometimes the branches break. On arrival, they go into hibernation for several months until the temperature starts to rise. Then they take to the skies in thick orange clouds, searching for milkweed plants on which to lay their eggs.

Milkweed munchers

Milkweed is vital to monarchs. It is the only thing their caterpillars eat. Milkweed also contains poisonous chemicals. These don't harm the caterpillar but make the butterfly poisonous to birds and mammals.

FACT: The viceroy butterfly has evolved to look

Life cycle of a monarch butterfly

1. The female lays her eggs on milkweed plants.

2. Four days later, the caterpillars hatch out and start feeding intensively for two weeks.

3. The caterpillar spins a silk pad on a leaf or twig and hangs upside down. Its skin splits to reveal a green chrysalis.

4. Inside the chrysalis, the caterpillar's body breaks down and reassembles itself into a butterfly.

5. The chrysalis splits and the butterfly wriggles out. It starts pumping fluid into its wings.

6. It hangs from the chrysalis for several hours until its wings become dry and stiff. It then flies away to feed.

Monarchs living on the west side of North America migrate to Southern California.

The original butterfly that migrated dies as it begins the return journey. It is the second, third, or even fourth generation of butterflies that eventually returns home. How they find their way back, having never made the trip before, is a mystery. Scientists think that their knowledge of the flight paths is inherited, and that they use the position of the Sun to work out their route.

Millions of butterflies travel thousands of miles to Mexico.

main **threats**

Monarchs are not endangered, but the Mexican trees they roost in are threatened by illegal logging. Large areas of the forest are now protected sites and logging has dropped by half. A butterfly reserve has been set up to attract tourists and provide an income for local people that will help preserve the forest.

like the monarch to stop predators from eating it.

Saving species

Some animals are SO CLOSE **to extinction** that **DESPERATE MEASURES** are called for. This is where **science** and **direct intervention** can come to the rescue. This is how ONE species was brought back from the brink.

Black-footed ferrets are members of the weasel family. They were once found all over the grasslands of North America, feeding on prairie dogs and living in their burrows. But when farmers began to wipe out prairie dogs, ferret numbers plummeted.

Black-footed **ferret**

Head count!
There were only **18** ferrets left before they were taken into captivity.

Rounding them up
When the numbers of a wild animal get too low, taking the survivors into captivity can be the best solution. This has happened to several species, including the black-footed ferret. With only 18 animals left, the ferret was facing extinction through a combination of disease and the extermination of its main food supply, prairie dogs. In 1987, the last wild ferrets were captured and a breeding program was set up to save them from extinction.

Prairie dogs are vital to the survival of the ferrets.

A bit of help
Breeding animals in captivity is not easy. The animals are not in their natural habitat, so the breeding pairs may not mate successfully and may need help to produce young. Scientists ensure that the best animals are mated and sometimes swap them between the breeding centers.

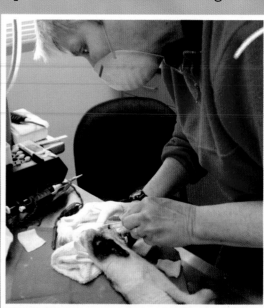

FACT: The black-footed ferret has now gone from

Ferret facts
Black-footed ferrets grow up to 2 ft (60 cm) long, nose-to-tail, and weigh around 2¼ lb (1 kg). They live for between three and five years.

Vital differences

One of the problems with a small population of animals is that only a few of them are the right age for breeding. Another problem is that the animals can become genetically almost identical. The health of a species depends on accidental changes to the genes (the set of instructions that determine an animal's structure and behavior) and the passing of good genes down the generations. Some genetic diversity is always needed in a species if the animals are to be different enough in tiny ways to survive and adapt to changing conditions.

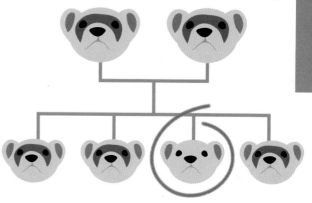

When animals produce babies, each of the offspring receives a mixed set of genes from its parents. Sometimes this mixing produces a random difference that may prove useful to the survival of the species.

SUCCESS!

There are now around 1,000 ferrets living on 17 reserves. Before they are released they are taught how to catch prairie dogs and vaccinated against plague and distemper, the two diseases that almost wiped them out. Every year, up to 250 new ferrets are returned to the wild.

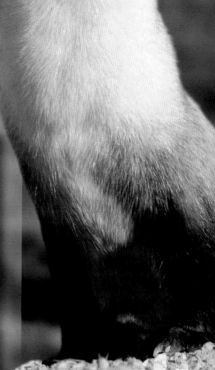

Back to the wild

By 1991, there were enough ferrets to start releasing them back into the wild. However, the scientists first had to make sure that there was an area where they could be released that had the right habitat and plenty of prairie dogs.

being classified as extinct in the wild to endangered.

Tracking tigers

Trying to find out how many animals of a particular species exist is a **tricky business**, even when they are as **LARGE** as a tiger. Only 3,200 tigers are thought to be alive in the wild. But there are still places where these secretive creatures **remain hidden** from human eyes.

Territory fit for tigers

Setting up a sanctuary

Tiger habitat has been shrinking into smaller and smaller pockets of land. Conservationists are trying to protect tigers by connecting these areas so that tigers can move between them in safety. There is a plan to set up a tiger corridor in the foothills of the Himalayas stretching from Nepal to Burma. First, scientists have to find out whether these areas are suitable for tigers. Little was known about wild tigers in Bhutan, so an expedition set out to search for them.

China

Himalayas

Nepal

Bhutan

Burma

Proposed corridor

India

Historic range
Current range

Tigers were once found across most of Asia but have been driven from 93% of their range.

FACT: The name "tiger" comes from the Persian word for

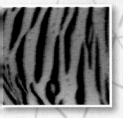
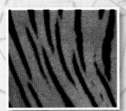

Tiger stripes

To count tigers accurately, scientists make a note of their side stripes. Each tiger has a slightly different pattern that can be photographed and stored in a database. Scientists can then check which tiger is crossing in front of the camera.

A tiger checking for scent marks.

Mountain cat

Tigers prefer to live in forested areas, but in Bhutan there were rumors that they were living high in the mountains. This is unusual, but remote cameras caught a male tiger scent-marking and a female who showed signs of having cubs. The footage proved that tigers were living and breeding at high altitudes. There were also tigers living in the foothills. If the corridor can be set up, Bhutan will be the stronghold from which tigers can spread out into neighboring countries.

Tiger **checklist**

There are a number of key things that scientists have to check before they can decide whether an area is suitable for a tiger corridor:

Assess the suitability of the habitat—is it a place where tigers could live?

Find out what other species live there and whether the ecosystem is healthy.

Find out from local people where and when tigers have been seen.

Look for evidence that tigers live there, for example, droppings, paw marks, and the remains of tiger kills.

Set up cameras to record how many tigers there are and where they are.

Find out whether there are enough prey animals to support the tigers.

Keeping animals alive

Protecting our wildlife is important to the health of the planet. There are **groups and organizations** all around the **WORLD** that are devoted to KEEPING **threatened species alive**. The key to many rescue efforts lies in **protecting** habitats and maintaining a **healthy number** of animals.

What does it take **to save our wildlife?**

Keep it natural

Many countries have areas that are protected as national parks or reserves. This allows animals to remain in their natural habitat without too much interference from humans. However, the areas often need to be monitored to make sure that no illegal activities such as logging or poaching are taking place. Sometimes the reserve has to be managed to make sure the habitat remains suitable for the species that live there.

Breeding programs

With some animals, such as the golden lion tamarin, breeding programs help boost numbers and stop tiny populations from becoming extinct. These are often set up in zoos or sanctuaries. Some of the animals are then released back into the wild, usually to a protected site, and are carefully looked after.

Relocation

Sometimes species have to be removed from their usual habitat and taken somewhere that is safer. In New Zealand, a group of kakapos (flightless parrots) has been moved to a small island that is free from predators that eat the birds and their eggs.

Captive breeding has increased the numbers of Przewalski's horses from 31 to around 1,500 animals.

FACT: Around 9,000 animals have been given a

This takes **effort** and **cooperation** from everyone involved—governments, wildlife experts, and interested **people like you.**

Staying healthy

Disease can devastate animal populations, especially among threatened species. In some cases, the disease is introduced by a related species. Ethiopian wolves can pick up illnesses from domestic dogs, so in areas where they are at risk, all the affected species are rounded up and vaccinated.

Legal protection

Preserving biodiversity is so important that almost every country has made laws to protect its wildlife and habitats. There are also international laws to protect species and habitats that cross national borders, and to prevent illegal trade in live animals and animal products.

Conservation organizations

Some of the biggest campaigns to save species are carried out by national and international organizations, such as the IUCN (International Union for Conservation of Nature), the WWF, Conservation International, and Bird Life International. They get actively involved with conserving species or help governments make agreements that will lead to the protection of a species.

Nature reserves aren't only found on land—many areas of the ocean have been made into protected sites to conserve species that live in the sea.

threatened classification on the IUCN's Red List.

You, too, can do your part to save wildlife. You don't even need to join a special group or travel overseas—you can start in your own backyard. After all, this is your habitat, too.

Tools of the trade

Every naturalist needs a good identification guide to help them put a name to their finds. A magnifying glass is useful for looking at small creatures, and binoculars can help you to observe shy animals that don't let humans get too close. Glass jars make great temporary specimen tanks, and a small net is ideal for sampling ponds or catching butterflies.

Check out the species

Keep a log of everything that comes into your yard—mammals, birds, reptiles, amphibians, and insects. Search the places where animals could be hiding, such as under dead logs, in piles of leaves, or in the branches of bushes. Make a record of where and when you saw each animal so that you can tell whether they are seasonal visitors or local residents.

MON: fox print

TUES: grass snake

WEDS: chickadee, sparrow

THURS: cat, ladybugs

FRI: 2 beetles, pigeon

Who's hiding behind this pile of leaves?

Tracking

There are some visitors that only enter your yard while you are asleep. Many animals prefer to look for food at night because it is safer, but you can figure out where these mysterious visitors have been if you look out for their tracks in soft soil, sand, or snow.

Dog family
Dogs and foxes have claws on each of their four toes.

Cat family
Cat prints show four symmetrical toe pads but no claw marks.

Mustelid family
Badger, weasel, and otter tracks show five toes and clear claw marks.

Rodent family
Rodents have four long toes on their front feet and five on their back.

FACT: Yards provide important habitats and

Identification guide

Glass jars

Binoculars

Magnifying glass

Net

Quadrats

You can use the same techniques that conservationists use to study the animal life in your own backyard. Why not try making your own quadrat sampler? You will need four pieces of plant stake, each measuring 3 ft (1 m) long. Or get a 12 ft (4 m) piece of string, knot it together, and hold it in place using a stick at each corner.

Place the frame on the ground and record the position of every creature you see inside. Repeat in the same place every few weeks to see what's new.

Conservation organizations

These organizations can offer more help and advice on conserving wildlife.

www.worldwildlife.org

www.nwf.org

www.wcs.org

feeding stations for your local wildlife.

Setting up a reserve

Now that you know what's living in your BACKYARD, there are various things you can do to turn this green patch into a **sanctuary** for wildlife. And, once you've realized which animals don't pay you a visit, you can also work out how to make your yard into a much more **tempting destination**.

Amphibian apartment

Amphibians like living in damp, shady places, and a clay flowerpot turned on its side makes a cool pad for frogs, toads, newts, and salamanders.

1 Find a cool, shady place in the yard and dig out a little hollow. Lay a clay flowerpot down here on its side.

2 Half fill the pot with soil and furnish your amphibian home with some damp leaves.

3 Using a hose or watering can, wet the area to keep it damp and to secure the loose soil in place.

4 Provide a small saucer of water for your amphibian guests to splash around in. Weigh it down with a little gravel to stop it from tipping over.

Ladybug sanctuary

Gardeners love ladybugs because they provide excellent natural pest control. Encourage them to hibernate over winter with this ingenious insect aviary.

1 Take a sheet of corrugated cardboard and cut a long strip that runs across all the dips and ridges.

2 Cut the top off a plastic drinks bottle. Roll up the strip of cardboard and gently tuck it into the cylinder.

3 Poke some twigs down into the roll of cardboard. These will make good landing posts for your ladybugs.

4 Find a dry, sheltered spot for the house, among the branches of a thick conifer or shrub. Tilt the bottle slightly downward so that it won't fill with water when it rains.

Going wild

If you want to encourage wildlife to visit your yard, you've got to make sure that you have a variety of habitats on offer. Trees and shrubs are good places for birds and insects to hide, and those that produce fruit or seeds are a

Hedges provide important food, shelter, and nesting sites for backyard wildlife.

valuable source of food. You could also try persuading your parents to let a small area of the yard go wild—weeds such as nettles, brambles, ivy, and wildflowers provide food and shelter for many animals.

Bee bivouac

Not all bees live in hives. Some are solitary and like to hide in cracks in walls and hollow plant stems over the winter.

1 Collect some short plant stakes or bamboo. Form into a bundle and secure with strong adhesive tape.

2 Press the bundle into a big lump of modeling clay. This will seal off one end of the hollow stalks.

3 Wedge the bundle into a plant pot. The clay should be at the bottom and the open stalk ends pointing outward.

4 Leave the bivouac in a dry, sunny spot for solitary bees to find. They can slip down the hollow stalks and shelter during the winter months.

Watch the birdy

Birds are a colorful addition to any yard. Encourage them to visit yours by putting out food, especially in the winter.

1 Take a clean, empty juice carton and cut out a hole about 2 in (5 cm) from the bottom of the container.

2 Decorate the bird feeder with a collage of leaf shapes cut from plastic bags and stuck in place with craft glue.

3 Carefully poke some small holes through the bottom of the carton. These will allow rainwater to drain out.

4 Poke a twig through the carton just beneath the food hole. This will form a handy perch. Fill the feeder with bird seed and hang with garden wire.

New species

Planet Earth still holds some SURPRISES for scientists prepared to journey to remote and unexplored places. Even though we have been SEARCHING FOR and **identifying species** for a few **HUNDRED** years, there are many that have gone **undetected** and **unrecorded**.

Around **18,000** new species are discovered each year. That's more than **two** species every hour!

Every year, scientists are **discovering** THOUSANDS of new creatures. In 2006, it was estimated that as many as **50 new species** were being discovered EVERY DAY.

650 new species have been found living near hot water vents under the ocean.

Many of these are invertebrates or live in the ocean. A 10-year survey of the ocean has revealed **5,000 new species**. It is estimated that there may be as many as a MILLION species in the ocean, and that we have only discovered **20 percent** of them so far.

In 2009, approximately **850 new species** of invertebrate were found in caves in the Australian Outback.

It isn't hard to miss a **tiny creature** hidden in the undergrowth, but some of the **most recent** discoveries are **MUCH BIGGER** than anyone expected. In recent years, several MONKEYS, a miniature **deer**, a **wallaby**, and a **tree kangaroo** have been found.

Researchers have identified 209 new species of Turbonilla sea snail. All of them are less than ½ in (1 cm) long.

"WE DON'T KNOW FOR SURE HOW MANY SPECIES THERE ARE, WHERE THEY CAN BE FOUND OR HOW FAST THEY'RE DISAPPEARING. IT'S LIKE HAVING ASTRONOMY WITHOUT KNOWING WHERE THE STARS ARE."

E. O. Wilson

FACT: Scientists estimate that the weight of all the

Rat as big as a CAT

Rain forests are good hunting grounds for new species. In 2009, an expedition to an ancient volcanic crater in Papua New Guinea filmed a ratlike animal that scientists thought could be a new species. Expert trackers managed to find a live specimen. The Bosavi woolly rat (right), as it is currently known, is completely unafraid of humans because it rarely comes into contact with them.

Already threatened

Sometimes species aren't discovered because they live in very remote or small habitats. The gray-faced sengi (left) was found in Tanzania in 2008 and is already classed as vulnerable. Although the two tiny areas of mountain forest where it lives are protected, its habitat is being reduced by bushfires and humans moving into the area.

Local secret

Sometimes "new" species are not so new to the local people. When scientists came across a 6 ft (2 m) long bitatawa monitor lizard walking across a field in the Philippines in 2010, they found that it was regularly hunted by the local people. Despite its bright blue, yellow, and green skin, the scientists had missed it because it rarely comes down from the trees.

Rain forests

Rain forests are some of the most impenetrable yet biodiverse areas on Earth, so it is not surprising that many new species are found there. Visits to the Foja Mountains in Indonesia have revealed many new animals, including this long-nosed frog (right), nicknamed the Pinocchio frog, and the golden-mantled tree kangaroo (left).

Oceans

The oceans are the most unexplored part of our planet. The deep sea is a hostile place for humans, yet millions of different animals have adapted to the conditions and made their homes there. The majority of new finds are crustaceans (crabs, lobsters, shrimp), mollusks (squid, clams, snails), but also as many as 136 new fish species (such as Satomi's pygmy seahorse and the psychedelic frogfish, left) are discovered every year.

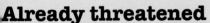

microbes in the ocean equals that of 240 billion African elephants!

Glossary

adaptation A special feature of an animal or plant that helps it to survive and reproduce in its environment.

algae Simple, nonflowering plants. Seaweeds are algae.

amphibian A cold-blooded animal that can live on land and in water.

aquatic Living in or near water.

biodiversity The number and variety of species living in a particular place.

breed To produce babies (young or offspring).

camouflage The way an animal is disguised so that it blends in with its surroundings.

carnivore An animal that eats meat.

climate The weather conditions that are usual for an area over a long time.

colony A group of animals living closely together or joined together in a structure. Corals live in colonies.

competition Competing demand between two or more animal species for the same food, shelter, or habitat.

conservation The protection of the natural environment and the wildlife that lives there.

crustacean An animal that has a hard shell, a pair of limbs on each body segment, and two pairs of antennae.

deforestation The cutting down of forests so that the land can be used either for crops, rearing livestock, homes, or roads.

dominant The most important or powerful animal in a group.

ecosystem Plants and animals that live together in a particular environment.

endangered Likely to become extinct.

environment The surroundings in which an animal lives.

evolution An idea developed by scientist Charles Darwin. It states that over many millions of years, living things change through natural selection to become more suited to a particular environment.

exoskeleton A hard, outer covering that protects an animal's body.

extinction The disappearance of a species or a population, so there are none left alive.

fossil The ancient remains of an animal or plant embedded in rock.

genes Part of a body cell. They pass on body features and characteristics between a parent and its offspring.

habitat The place or environment where an animal naturally lives.

herbivore An animal that eats only plants.

hibernation The ability of some animals to slow their bodily activities down for a time, so they appear to be in a deep sleep. Animals usually hibernate during the colder months when food is scarce.

hybrid The offspring of two living things that belong to different breeds or species.

interbreed The mating or breeding of one animal with an animal from a related breed or species. Dogs and wolves are different species but can interbreed.

introduced species An animal that lives in an area where it is not naturally found, brought in by people either on purpose, perhaps to prey on pests or as a pet, or accidentally.

invertebrate An animal without a backbone.

keratin A tough fiber that forms an animal's hair, fur, claws, horns, hooves, or feathers. Rhino horns look like bone but are made of keratin.

livestock Animals that are raised by people for a purpose, such as farm animals that are raised for food.

mammal A warm-blooded animal that has hair or fur and feeds its young milk. Most give birth to live young.

marsupial A mammal that gives birth to underdeveloped young, which it then carries in a pouch.

migrate To move from one area to another to breed or feed, at a set time every year.

natural selection The process whereby some animals that are better suited to their environment than others tend to survive and produce more offspring.

offspring An animal's baby. Also called young.

pollution The existence of dangerous or unpleasant objects or substances in a natural environment.

population The number of animals, or species of animal, living in a particular place.

predator An animal that kills and eats other animals.

prey An animal that is hunted and killed by another for food.

range The areas where an animal lives in the world.

reptile A cold-blooded animal that has scaly skin. The majority lay soft-shelled eggs on land.

scavenger An animal that feeds on animals that have been killed by others.

species A group of living things that share similar characteristics, such as shape, size, and coloring.

territory The area of land where an animal or group of animals live. They defend this area from different species or from members of the same species and gender.

vertebrate An animal with a backbone.

Index

adaptation 5, 7, 12, 14, 66
agriculture 14, 19, 22, 39, 56
albatross 59
algae 30, 62
amphibians 4, 6, 15, 47, 52–53, 72, 74
ant 19, 60
Asian crested ibis 39
axolotl 53

backyards 72–75
Bali starling 38
bear
   black bear 19, 42
   grizzly bear 10, 11
   Malayan Sun bear 16
   polar bear 34–35
beaver 10, 11
bees 15, 75
beluga sturgeon 57
bilby 18
biodiversity 8–9, 71, 77
birds 7, 13, 38–39, 72, 75
black stilt 38
blue whale 18
Bosavi woolly rat 77
breeding programs 39, 42, 44, 51, 52,
   66, 70
bushfires 15, 19, 51, 53
bushmeat 14, 18

camouflage 21
captivity 15, 17, 19, 27, 39, 51, 52, 66
cat 13, 39, 47, 72
chimpanzee 16
climate change 12, 14, 15, 19, 34, 39,
   40, 46, 47, 53, 61, 62
competition 5, 7, 32, 38, 40, 47, 61
conservation 27, 36, 37, 44, 51, 71, 73
coral 6, 8, 60, 62–63
corridors 22–23, 68–69
coyote 10, 11
crocodile 46
crustaceans 60, 63

dams 38, 52, 53, 57
Darwin, Charles 6, 7
Darwin's frog 52
deer 11, 51
deforestation 19, 39, 52, 53
desert 4, 14, 60
development 30, 49, 53, 60
dinosaur 7
disease 5, 15, 16, 18, 28, 29, 32, 47, 66,
   67, 71
dodo 13
dog 13, 28, 47, 71, 72
dugong 31

earthquakes 15, 51
ecosystems 8–9, 10, 11, 27, 47, 53, 54, 66

elephant 77
elk 10, 11
evolution 6–7
extinction 12–13, 14, 19, 47, 54, 66

ferret 66–67
fish 6, 11, 39, 46, 48, 56–57, 63, 77
flooding 15, 38
food 4, 8, 14, 15, 34, 35, 39, 40, 41, 51
food chain 11, 15
fossils 7, 13, 44
fox 16, 32, 33, 39, 42, 72
frog 7, 52–53, 77

Galápagos 7, 47
genes 67
gharial 46
golden lion tamarin 70
golden-mantled tree kangaroo 77
golden toad 54–55
gorilla 16
gray-faced sengi 77

habitat 4, 11, 16, 17, 18, 19, 22, 23, 53,
   66, 70, 72, 75
habitat loss 14, 15, 19, 20, 22, 23, 24,
   28, 36, 38, 39, 42, 47, 51, 61
hotspots 9
hunting 10, 11, 13, 14, 18, 19, 24, 25,
   26, 30, 32, 36, 47, 49, 51, 52
hyacinth macaw 39

illegal trade 23, 24, 34, 37, 71
Indian vulture 38
insects 5, 7, 60, 72, 75
introduced species 18, 19, 33, 38, 39, 46,
   47, 60, 61
invasive species 47, 61
invertebrates 5, 6, 60–61

jaguar 20–21, 22–23

kakapo 17, 70
keystone species 27
komodo dragon 50–51

ladybug 74
land clearance 22, 24, 28, 36, 39, 51
lizards 46, 50–51, 77
logging 18, 39, 65, 70

mammals 7, 18, 72
manatee 30–31
marsupials 18, 32
migration 4, 34, 44–45, 61, 64–65
mollusks 6
monarch butterfly 64–65
monitor lizard 77

natural hazards 15, 51

ocean 9, 18, 48, 76, 77
oil spills 26, 34, 47, 57, 58
orangutan 24–25
oryx 19
overfishing 9, 39, 40, 41, 57, 58, 59, 61

penguin 39, 40–41
pet trade 14, 25, 38, 39, 46, 47, 53,
   57, 61
platypus 18
poaching 20, 23, 24, 25, 36, 37, 51, 70
poison 18, 30, 32, 34, 63
pollution 9, 14, 15, 18, 26, 34, 47, 49,
   52, 53, 57, 58, 61, 62
prairie dog 66, 67
predators 10, 11, 20, 26, 38, 39, 40,
   42, 70
protection 18, 49, 51, 60, 65, 70, 71

rain forest 8, 9, 20, 22, 23, 52, 62, 77
rat 13, 39, 47, 77
reintroduced species 10, 27, 67, 70
reptiles 4, 6, 7, 46–47, 72
reserves 9, 65, 67, 70
rhinoceros 36–37
risk categories (IUCN) 16–17
rodent 72

salamander 52
sanctuaries 25, 68, 70, 74
scavengers 10, 38
sea otter 26–27
sea urchin 26, 27
seal 17, 34, 35, 40
shark 6, 56
shelter 4, 14, 25
snail 60, 76
snake 46
spider 60, 61

Tasmanian devil 32–33
threats 14–15, 16, 17
tiger 5, 68–69
toad 52, 54, 55
tortoise 17, 47
tracking 68–69, 72
traditional medicine 14, 19, 36, 47
tuatara 46
turtle 46, 47, 48, 49

vertebrates 5, 52, 56

weasel 72
whooping crane 42–45
wolf 42
   Ethiopian wolf 28–29, 71
   gray wolf 10
worms 6, 60, 61

zoos 70

Acknowledgments

Dorling Kindersley would like to thank Fleur Star for her editorial help with this book.

The publisher would like to thank the following for their kind permission to reproduce their photographs:

(Key: a-above; b-below/bottom; c-center; f-far; l-left; r-right; t-top)

1 Getty Images: Martin Barraud (c/main image). **1–11 Getty Images:** Garry Gay (t/map background). **4 Corbis:** Aso Fujita/Amanaimages (tr). **Getty Images:** Steve Allen/The Image Bank (crb); Daniel J. Cox/Photographer's Choice (cb); Tim Flach (clb). **4–5 Getty Images:** Dieter Spears/iStock Exclusive (b/green background). **5 Getty Images:** Matthias Breiter/Minden Pictures (cb); Andy Rouse/The Image Bank (crb); Jonathan & Angela Scott/The Image Bank (clb); Jami Tarris/Botanica (t). **6 Alamy Images:** PHOTOTAKE Inc./Dennis Kunkel Microscopy, Inc. (bl/bacteria). **Reproduced with permission from John van Wyhe ed., The Complete Work of Charles Darwin Online (http://darwin-online.org.uk/):** (ca/frogs), (cra/cicada). **Science Photo Library:** (cr); Lynette Cook (fbl). **7 Corbis:** Buddy Mays (ca/frog). **Reproduced with permission from John van Wyhe ed., The Complete Work of Charles Darwin Online (http://darwin-online.org.uk/):** (tl/finches). **8 Corbis:** Kulka (clb) (fcla/leaf); Paul Souders (bl). **Getty Images:** Steve Allen/Brand X Pictures (bc) (fbr). **Science Photo Library:** Georgette Douwma (crb). **9 Corbis:** Anthony Bannister/Gallo Images (clb/bl image in jigsaw); Frans Lanting (clb/tr image in jigsaw); Momatiuk - Eastcott (bc); Patrick Robert/Sygma (clb/tc image in jigsaw); Tom Soucek/Verge (clb/br image in jigsaw); Paul Souders (t/leaf); Scott Stulberg (clb/bc image in jigsaw). **Getty Images:** Danita Delimont/Gallo Images (clb/tl image in jigsaw); David Edwards/National Geographic (br); Pete Oxford/Minden Pictures (tr/macaw). **iStockphoto.com:** Will Evans (cr/map). **10 Dorling Kindersley:** Dudley Edmonson (c). **10–11 Getty Images:** James Randklev (c/landscape background); Dieter Spears/iStock Exclusive (beige & green text backgrounds). **11 Getty Images:** Daniel J. Cox/Photographer's Choice (tl) (cl) (cr); Raymond Gehman/National Geographic (cra); James Hager/Robert Harding World Imagery (cla); Norbert Rosing/National Geographic (crb). **12 Corbis:** (cl); Martin Rietze/Moodboard (bl). **12–13 Getty Images:** The Bridgeman Art Library/Royal Albert Memorial Museum, Exeter, Devon (dodo). **iStockphoto.com:** Peter Berko (b/beige footer). **13 Corbis:** Kevin Schafer (tl). **14–15 Getty Images:** Garry Gay (t/map background); Dieter Spears/iStock Exclusive (beige paper texture background). **15 Getty Images:** Rich Reid/National Geographic (t/main photo). **16 Corbis:** Steve Kaufman (cla). **Getty Images:** Cyril Ruoso/JH Editorial/Minden Pictures (br). **naturepl.com:** Eric Baccega (bc). **NHPA/Photoshot:** Nigel J. Dennis (bl). **16–17 iStockphoto.com:** Peter Berko (colored text boxes). **17 Corbis:** John Carnemolla (br); Malte Christians/EPA (bc); Frans Lanting (bl). **naturepl.com:** ARCO (cra); Andrew Walmsley (tl). **18 Corbis:** Frans Lanting (clb); Denis Scott (crb). **naturepl.com:** Dave Watts (cb). **18–19 Getty Images:** Dieter Spears/iStock Exclusive (b/green background). **18–22 Getty Images:** Garry Gay (t/map background). **19 Corbis:** Tom Brakefield (crb); DLILLC (cra); Steve Kaufman (clb). **Getty Images:** C. Dani-I . Jeske/De Agostini Picture Library (cb). **20 Ardea:** Thomas Marent (cla). **20–21 Corbis:** W. Perry Conway (main image). **21 Alamy Images:** Paris Pierce (tl). **Getty Images:** Brian Kenney (tc). **iStockphoto.com:** Will Evans (crb/map). **22 Corbis:** Rickey Rogers/Reuters (cla). **Getty Images:** Stephen Ferry/Liaison (clb). **NHPA/Photoshot:** Andy Rouse (br); Kevin Schafer (main image). **23 Corbis:** Steve Kaufman (cla); R H Productions/Robert Harding World Imagery (clb). **NHPA/Photoshot:** Andy Rouse. **24 Ardea:** Jean Paul Ferrero (bc). **Getty Images:** Photo 24/Brand X Pictures (cla). **24–25 Corbis:** DLILLC (main image). **24–44 Getty Images:** Garry Gay (t/map background). **25 Corbis:** Frans Lanting (tc). **FLPA:** Colin Marshall (bl). **iStockphoto.com:** Will Evans (crb/map). **OnAsia:** Oka Budhi (br). **26 iStockphoto.com:** Will Evans (crb/map). **naturepl.com:** Tom Mangelsen (cla). **26–27 Corbis:** Steven Kazlowski/Science Faction (main image). **Getty Images:** Dieter Spears/iStock Exclusive (b/beige footer). **27 Corbis:** AlaskaStock (cla); Jonathan Blair (ca); Christie's Images (tl); Frans Lanting (cra). **iStockphoto.com:** Emmanouil Gerasidis (tr). **28 Corbis:** Martin Harvey (cla). **28–29 NHPA/Photoshot:** Martin Harvey (main image). **29 Ardea:** M. Watson (tl). **Corbis:** Martin Harvey/Gallo Images (cla). **iStockphoto.com:** Will Evans (br/map). **naturepl.com:** Laurent Geslin (ca) (cra) (tc). **30 Corbis:** Bettmann (cla). **iStockphoto.com:** Will Evans (bc/map). **30–31 Getty Images:** Carol Grant/Flickr (main image). **31 Getty Images:** De Agostini Picture Library (tl) (crb); Brian J. Skerry/National Geographic (tc). **32 Getty Images:** Kathie Atkinson/Photolibrary (cla); Dave Walsh/Flickr (crb). **32–33 Photolibrary:** J. & C. Sohns/Picture Press (main image). **33 iStockphoto.com:** Will Evans (crb/map). **34 Getty Images:** Henrik Winther Andersen/Flickr (cla). **34–35 Science Photo Library:** Thomas Nilsen (main image). **35 Corbis:** Steven Kazlowski/Science Faction (tc). **Getty Images:** Daniel J. Cox/Photographer's Choice (br). **iStockphoto.com:** Will Evans (crb/map). **NHPA/Photoshot:** John Shaw (ca). **36 Corbis:** Kevin Schafer (cla). **iStockphoto.com:** Will Evans (crb/map). **36-37 NHPA/Photoshot:** Martin Harvey (main image). **37 NHPA/Photoshot:** Daryl Balfour (cb); Tony Crocetta (crb); Steve & Ann Toon (tc). **38 naturepl.com:** Tony Heald (cb); Tom Marshall (crb); David Tipling (clb). **38–39 Getty Images:** Dieter Spears/iStock Exclusive (b/blue background). **39 Corbis:** Martin Harvey (cb); Bob Jacobson (t/main image). **iStockphoto.com:** Peter Berko (cr/text box). **Photolibrary:** imagebroker RF (crb); Panorama Stock RF (clb). **40 Corbis:** Roger Tidman (cla). **NHPA/Photoshot:** Rich Kirchner (cra). **40–41 FLPA:** Tui De Roy/Minden Pictures (main image). **41 iStockphoto.com:** Will Evans (crb/map). **NHPA/Photoshot:** Mike Lane (tc). **42 iStockphoto.com:** Will Evans (crb/map). **SuperStock:** James Urbach (cla). **42–43 Alamy Images:** Mike Briner (main image). **43 Getty Images:** Arthur Morris/Visuals Unlimited (tc). **44 Corbis:** Chris Baltimore/Reuters (cla). **naturepl.com:** Mark Payne-Gill (main image). **45 Alamy Images:** Danita Delimont (clb). **naturepl.com:** Tom Hugh-Jones (main image); Thomas Lazar (cla). **46 Corbis:** Michael & Patricia Fogden (clb); Sanjeev Gupta/EPA (cb); Frans Lanting (crb). **46–47 Getty Images:** Dieter Spears/iStock Exclusive (b/green background). **46–71 Getty Images:** Garry Gay (t/map background). **47 Corbis:** Ira Block/National Geographic Society (crb); Guillermo Granja/Reuters (cb); David A. Northcott (clb). **Getty Images:** Joseph Van Os/The Image Bank (tr/main image). **iStockphoto.com:** Peter Berko (cra/text box). **48 Corbis:** Visuals Unlimited (bl); Kennan Ward (cla). **48–49 National Geographic Stock:** Bill Curtsinger. **49 Corbis:** Brian J. Skerry/National Geographic Society (fclb). **iStockphoto.com:** Will Evans (crb/map). **naturepl.com:** Solvin Zankl (clb). **scubazooimages.com:** Jason Isley (tc). **SuperStock:** National Geographic (cb). **50 Alamy Images:** WaterFrame (clb). **50–51 naturepl.com:** Visuals Unlimited (main image). **51 Alamy Images:** Wolfgang Kaehler (tc). **Getty Images:** Marvin E. Newman/Photographer's Choice (cb). **iStockphoto.com:** Will Evans (crb/map). **52 Ardea:** Ken Lucas (clb). **Corbis:** Michael & Patricia Fogden (crb). **Science Photo Library:** Dante Fenolio (cb). **52–53 Getty Images:** Dieter Spears/iStock Exclusive (b/green background). **53 FLPA:** Fabio Pupin (tr/main image). **NHPA/Photoshot:** Stephen Dalton (cb); Ken Griffiths (clb); Daniel Heuclin (crb). **54 Getty Images:** Michael & Patricia Fogden/Minden Pictures (cla). **54–55 Getty Images:** Michael & Patricia Fogden/Minden Pictures (main image). **55 Getty Images:** Michael & Patricia Fogden/Minden Pictures (tl) (cra). **iStockphoto.com:** Will Evans (clb/map). **NHPA/Photoshot:** David Woodfall (tc). **56 Corbis:** Amos Nachoum (clb). **Getty Images:** Fred Bavendam/Minden Pictures (cb); Purestock (crb). **56–57 Getty Images:** Dieter Spears/iStock Exclusive (b/blue background). **57 Corbis:** Ralph A. Clevenger (cb). **naturepl.com:** Nature Production (clb); Wild Wonders of Europe/Sá (tr/main image). **NHPA/Photoshot:** Franco Banfi (crb). **58 Alamy Images:** Mark Conlin/VWpics/Visual&Written SL (ca). **iStockphoto.com:** Will Evans (clb/map). **58–59 Getty Images:** Dieter Spears/iStock Exclusive (pink background). **naturepl.com:** Wild Wonders of Europe/Zankl (main image). **59 Getty Images:** Paul Sutherland/National Geographic (tl). **60 Ardea:** Pat Morris (cb). **Corbis:** Jeffrey L. Rotman (crb). **Visuals Unlimited, Inc.:** Alex Wild (clb). **60–61 Getty Images:** Dieter Spears/iStock Exclusive (b/beige background). **61 Alamy Images:** Michael Soo (cb). **Corbis:** Stefan Sollfors/Science Faction (crb). **naturepl.com:** Pete Oxford (tr/main image). **NHPA/Photoshot:** Anthony Bannister (clb). **62 Corbis:** Stuart Westmorland (cla). **OceanwideImages.com:** Gary Bell (bl). **62–63 OceanwideImages.com:** Gary Bell (main image). **62–73 iStockphoto.com:** Peter Berko (b/cream/beige background). **63 Alamy Images:** WaterFrame (cb/Antler coral). **Corbis:** Visuals Unlimited (clb/Fan coral); Lawson Wood (clb/Brain coral); Rungroj Yongrit/EPA (tr). **OceanwideImages.com:** (cr). **64 Corbis:** Image Source (cra); Frans Lanting (clb) (cr). **64–65 Corbis:** Radius Images (butterflies in blue sky). **65 Corbis:** Radius Images (tl/stage 3); Tom Van Sant/Geosphere (b/map). **Dorling Kindersley:** Natural History Museum, London (cb/butterflies over map). **naturepl.com:** Ingo Arndt (ftl/stage 1) (tc/stage 4) (tr/stage 5); Thomas Lazar (tr/stage 6); Visuals Unlimited (tl/stage 2). **66 Alamy Images:** m-images (tr). **Corbis:** Rick Wilking/Reuters (br). **Getty Images:** UVimages/amanaimages (bl). **naturepl.com:** Shattil & Rozinski (tl). **66–67 Alamy Images:** m-images (b/blurred background). **67 Corbis:** Jeff Vanuga (clb). **FLPA:** Sumio Harada/Minden Picture (tl). **naturepl.com:** Andrew Harrington (bc); Shattil & Rozinski (br). **68 Getty Images:** Planet Observer/Universal Images Group (main map image). **iStockphoto.com:** Will Evans (clb/map). **69 Corbis:** Frans Lanting (tl/2nd image from l). **naturepl.com:** Andy Rouse (l); Anup Shah (tr). **70–71 Getty Images:** Martin Barraud (main image). **72 Corbis:** Niall Benvie (crb/fox tracks); Tim Pannell (bc/leaves). **Getty Images:** Peter Mason (cla); Walter B. McKenzie (cra/beetle). **73 Corbis:** Chris Harris/First Light (tl/moon). **Getty Images:** Garry Gay (b/map background). **iStockphoto.com:** Peter Berko (clb/orange background). **Wikipedia, The Free Encyclopedia:** Yohan euan o4. From: http://commons.wikimedia.org/wiki/File:Quadrat_sample.JPG. Creative Commons Attribution-Share Alike 3.0 Unported licence: http://creativecommons.org/licenses/by-sa/3.0/deed.en (crb). **74–80 Getty Images:** Garry Gay (t/map background). **76 Corbis:** Frans Lanting (tr). **fotolia:** Elenathewise (bl/seashell background); Aleksandr Ugorenkov (clb/rock background). **Getty Images:** Tryman, Kentaroo/Johner Images (cla/water background). **76–80 iStockphoto.com:** Peter Berko (b/cream footer background). **77 Corbis:** Joseph Brown/University of Kansas/Reuters (cr); Francesco Rovero/California Academy of Sciences/Reuters (cla). **Getty Images:** Birgitte Wilms/Minden Pictures (bl/psychedelic frogfish). **Jonathan Keeling:** (tr). **National Geographic Stock:** Timothy G. Laman (crb). **NHPA/Photoshot:** Bruce Beehler (clb). **Wikipedia, The Free Encyclopedia:** John Sear. From: http://commons.wikimedia.org/wiki/File:Quadrat_sample.JPG. Creative Commons Attribution-Share Alike 3.0 Unported licence: http://creativecommons.org/licenses/by-sa/3.0/deed.en (fbl).

Jacket images: *Front:* **iStockphoto.com:** Andrey Ushakov. *Back:* **Dorling Kindersley:** Natural History Museum, London fcra; **FLPA:** Tui De Roy/Minden Pictures cra (penguins); **Getty Images:** Garry Gay t (map background); P. Jaccod/De Agostini Picture Library (main image); Tim Laman/National Geographic ca; Nick Gordon/Photolibrary cla.

All other images © Dorling Kindersley
For further information see: www.dkimages.com